BEAUTIFUL BUILDING BLOCK QUILTS

CREATE IMPROVISATIONAL QUILTS FROM ONE BLOCK • 8 PROJECTS • TIPS ON COLOR

Lisa Walton

C&T PUBLISHING

Text copyright © 2013 by Lisa Walton

How-To Photography and Artwork copyright © 2013 by C&T Publishing, Inc.

Quilt Photography copyright © 2013 by Andrew Payne of Photographix

Publisher: Amy Marson

Creative Director: Gailen Runge

Art Director: Kristy Zacharias

Editor: Cynthia Bix

Technical Editors: Teresa Stroin, Sadhana Wray, and Amanda Siegfried

Cover Designers: Kris Yenche and Kristy Zacharias

Book Designer: Rose Sheifer-Wright

Production Coordinator: Jenny Davis

Production Editors: S. Michele Fry and Joanna Burgarino

Illustrator: Jessica Jenkins

Photography Assistant: Cara Pardo

Photography by Christina Carty-Francis and Diane Pedersen of C&T Publishing, Inc., unless otherwise noted

Published by C&T Publishing, Inc., P.O. Box 1456, Lafayette, CA 94549

Library of Congress Cataloging-in-Publication Data

Walton, Lisa, 1956-

Beautiful building block quilts : create improvisational quilts from one block - 8 projects - tips on color / Lisa Walton.

pages cm

ISBN 978-1-60705-623-2 (soft cover)

1. Patchwork--Patterns. 2. Quilting--Patterns. I. Title.

TT835.W35657 2013

746.46'041--dc23

2012030337

Printed in China

10 9 8 7 6 5 4 3 2 1

Dedication

There is no way I could have done this book without the amazing support of my husband, Peter. He was there with meals when I needed them, the odd gin and tonic when I needed it, and a constant stream of positive reinforcement when it all got on top of me. He is my soul mate.

Acknowledgments

I would like to thank the following companies for their advice, support, and products that made my task a lot easier:

Aurifil for threads

Electric Quilt

Omnigrid for rulers, cutters, and mats

Pellon Products

Robert Kaufman Fabrics

Also I would like to give thanks to my friends who rallied around me when I needed encouragement and help.

Quilt photography by Andrew Payne of Photographix
www.photographix.com.au

Quilting by Kimpossible Quilting, unless otherwise noted
http://kimbradleycreations.com/

Contents

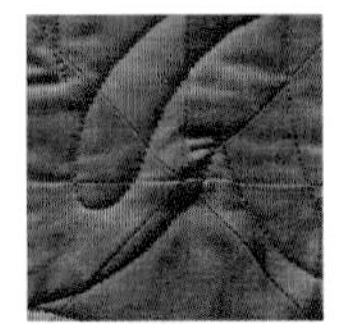

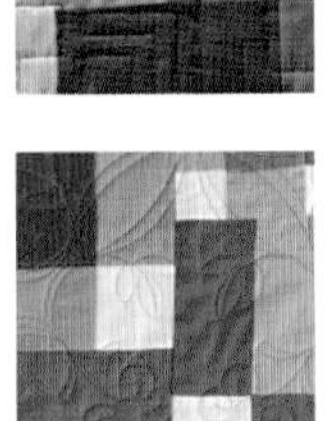

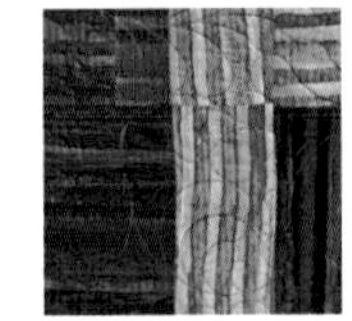
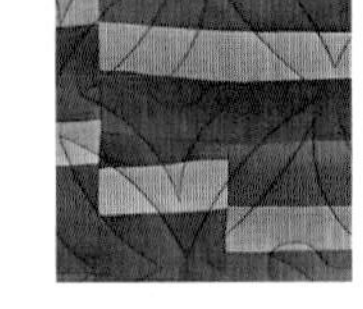

Introduction

I am lazy—I admit it! I cut corners, I hate following directions, and I am a dreadful student! So what am I doing here trying to tell you what to do?

Well, I love color and fabric and shapes, and putting them all together to make quilts is my passion. To top it off, I absolutely adore sharing my passion with others. The joy I get when teaching or showing students something and then seeing them grasp it and run with it is pure heaven.

The eight quilts in this book (and the bonus versions of four of them) are based on blocks made up of simple geometric shapes—squares, rectangles, and triangles. These blocks can be as simple as basic Four-Patch (four squares joined to make a larger square) designs or Flying Geese (three triangles joined to make a rectangle) designs. What makes the final quilt different is that instead of combining blocks of the same size (either different designs or all the same block), I create two or three size variations—multiples—of the basic block, combine them into larger units—modules—and eventually join these to create a unique quilt top.

The concept of using multiple sizes of the same block in a quilt has developed gradually over the years. I don't remember setting out to have a style or a technique but just noticed that a pattern was developing. I've always loved jigsaw puzzles, too, so maybe that was an influence.

Color and value, and how each is placed, are important aspects of what makes these quilts "sing." I am a fabric dyer as well as a quilt designer, and as you will see, the quilts in this book are created using hand-dyed fabrics as well as batiks and solids.

In this book I will show you how to plan both the colors and the design of your quilt by drawing a layout on graph paper or in a computer program such as Electric Quilt. From there, you'll see how to do some improvising and playing with the placement of elements until you are pleased with the layout.

I rarely know what a quilt is going to look like before I start, and it usually changes many times during its creation—but I love the process. I almost always start with a collection of fabrics and a vague idea of a design or shape of block, and just start cutting.

I make mistakes and miscalculations and run out of fabric regularly, but I usually find that it all works out well in the end. This serendipitous method of creating quilts may not work for everyone, but I assure you that after you give yourself permission to play, you will really enjoy the process and the quilts that result from it.

In this book, I have given you the basic concept and techniques for some quilts that you can really have fun with. I want you to take what you need to create your own designs and, of course, magnificent quilts. It doesn't matter if you make mistakes or run out of fabric or decide to change the design midway through the quilt. The most important ability I want you to get from this book is to be able to say, "I wonder what will happen if ...," and then just do it.

Four-Patch blocks in multiple sizes for *Power of Three* fit together in many combinations (full quilt on page 22).

Designing Your Own Blocks

Did you hate math in school, as I did? Did you think there would be no place in your future life that would use it in any shape or form? How wrong we were! As quilters we use numbers all the time, and although I don't think I will ever need to explore the inner depths of calculus, I really love playing with simple numbers now.

The designs in this book are based on basic arithmetic. By following the process in this book I am sure you will be able to create exciting and original designs from basic block designs.

1 + 1 = 2 2 + 2 = 4 4 + 4 = 8

Get the idea?

The Basics

Before you design your quilt, you will design the individual blocks, which you will then use to create modules, or groups of blocks. In turn, you will combine these modules into a quilt top.

Most basic geometric quilt block designs can be divided into 2″ or 3″ segments. Block sizes of 8″ and 9″ are common. You can combine an 8″ block with other blocks that are multiples of 2, such as 2″, 4″, and 6″ blocks. The 9″ blocks combine with multiples of 3, including 3″, 6″, and 12″ blocks. For example, a pair of 3″ blocks can be adjacent to a 6″ block and so on. Different-sized blocks are sewn together to create modules; then the modules can be repeated or different modules can be fitted together to create larger sections.

I try to avoid fractions in my designs. I like to be able to cut on those thick lines of my rulers, so I rarely design blocks or quilts that use eighth-inch (⅛″, ⅜″, ⅝″, or ⅞″) measurements. To avoid these fractional measurements, I look at the grid size of a proposed block.

Most blocks will fit in a grid of two, three, four, or nine equal units. You just need to look carefully at the block to work out how many of these equal units there are, and that will determine the grid size. The easiest way is to look at the top or the side of the block and count across or down. (There are of course many five- and seven-grid block designs, but once you start working with multiples of 5, such as 10″ and 15″ blocks, or 7, such as 14″ and 21″ blocks, it starts getting a little unwieldy.)

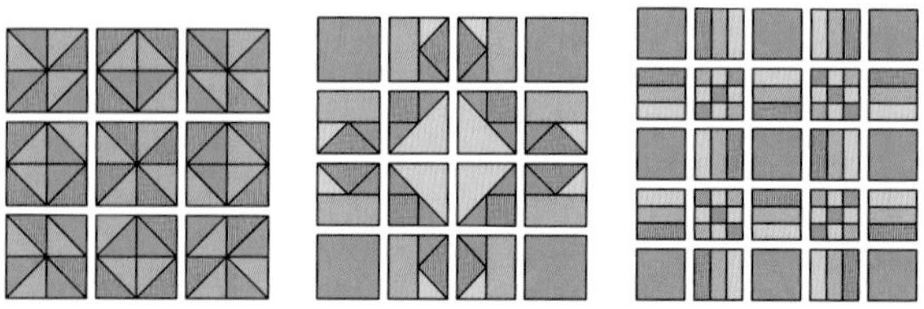

Three-Patch block

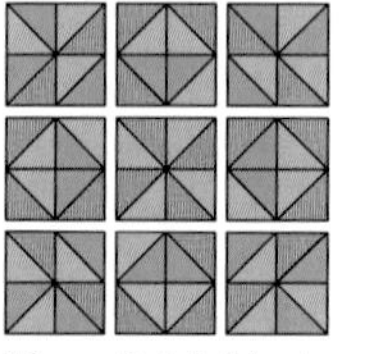

Four-Patch block

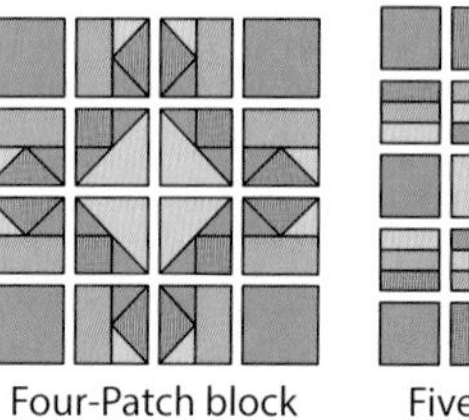

Five-Patch block

Variety of different block grids

If you are using a block whose grid is a multiple of 2, pick block sizes that are also multiples of 2 (4″, 6″, 8″, 10″, and 12″).

Some four-unit block options

Likewise, if you are using a block in which the grid is a multiple of 3, pick block sizes that are also multiples of 3 (6″, 9″, and 12″).

Some three-unit block options

After you work out the grid unit, draw the block in the largest size you would like. Then start adapting it to the different sizes you want. The new sizes of the block need to be a multiple of the size of the original block.

Block Design

The first step in designing your quilt is to select a block. There are so many books and magazines with blocks that you will never run out of ideas. The Internet is another brilliant resource.

Some block reference books available from Stash Books and C&T Publishing

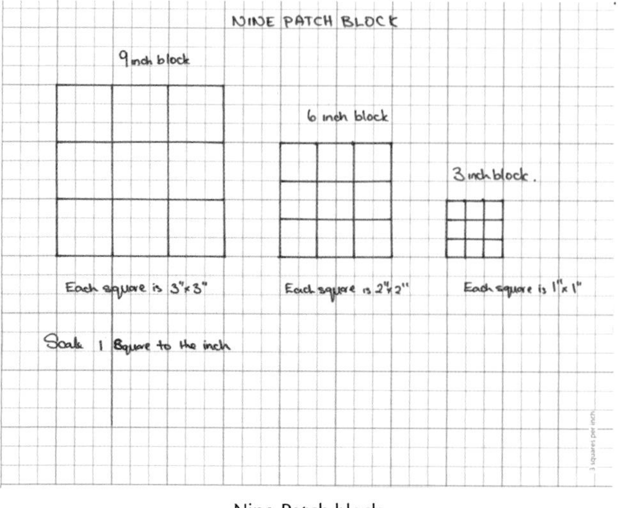

Nine-Patch block

Breaking down the designs: Nine-Patch block

I'll demonstrate the block design process with a very simple block.

You can draw blocks on graph paper or use a computer program such as Electric Quilt.

Using graph paper

Graph paper comes in many different sizes in both metric and American units. Since quilters tend to work with inches, I recommend selecting graph paper in a range of inch-based sizes. I use paper with three or nine squares to the inch for designs in which the block needs to be divided equally into three, six, or nine units. For designs in which the block will be divided equally into two, four, or eight units, I use paper with four or eight squares to the inch.

The Nine-Patch is a block of nine units, a three-grid, so I am using graph paper that is three squares to the inch. If the block size is larger than the scale of the graph paper, as in the case of the 9″ block I am drafting, it's best to draw the block smaller and to scale. So for this block, each square represents 1″.

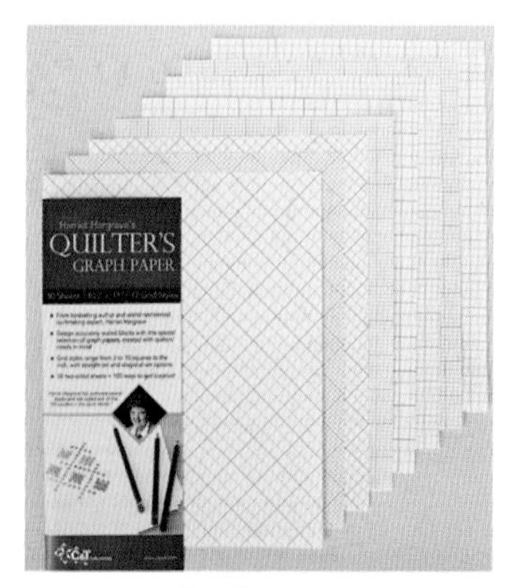

Graph papers

After you have established the block sizes, you can start playing with the combinations that will go together to make the larger modules. These modules will then be combined to make the quilt top.

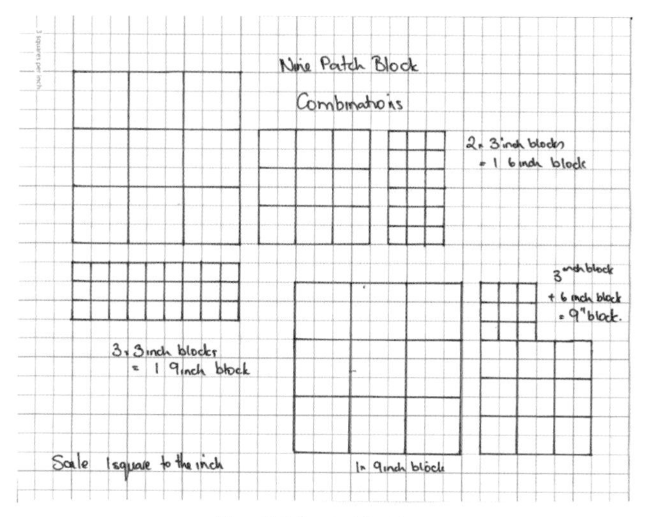

Nine-Patch combinations

Tip

You can buy graph paper in office supply and quilting stores. It is also available online with free downloads that allow you to customize the grid pattern of the graph specifically to your needs (see Resources, page 79).

Using quilt design software

I like to use Electric Quilt (EQ), a computer program that allows users to play around with designs and blocks in many different combinations and sizes. It is designed specifically for quilters, and includes a detailed user manual and excellent help videos. The website (see Resources, page 79) also is very user friendly and has a user forum.

The program also allows users to import fabric collections and incorporate them into quilt designs on the computer, creating an even better idea of what the final quilt is going to look like. Most of the quilts presented in this book are designed to be made from solids or hand-dyed fabrics, and EQ allowed me to use a solid color palette instead of prints for these designs.

As a quilt designer I love the ability to work "backward." Quite often my quilt designs develop as I work or change because of the very frequent mistakes I make. After I have finished making the quilt, I use EQ to calculate how much fabric I have used and to replicate interesting original designs that have developed.

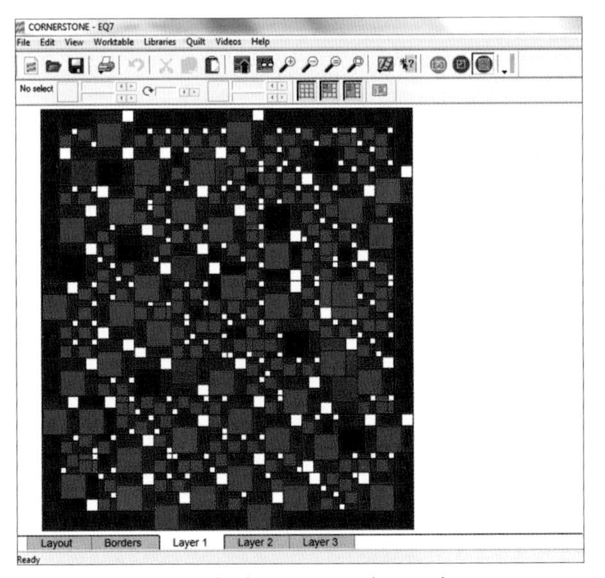

EQ draft of *Cornerstones* (page 48)

Proportion

Proportion is often quite important for designing a block in various sizes. In the example below, an 8″ block has a 1″ border or frame. If you add the same size border to a 4″ or 2″ version of the same block, the design won't work because of the proportions.

Play around with the border sizes and reduce them so that they look acceptable. You don't have to use perfect proportional calculations—but it should look good to you. The resulting blocks will have the same design but will work better with each other.

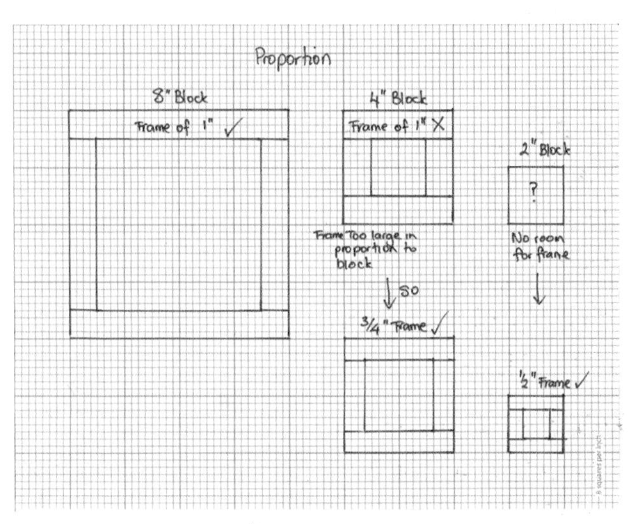

Working out proportions

Color and Fabrics

Understanding Color

Many excellent books explore using color and color theory. I find *Ultimate 3-in-1 Color Tool* by Joen Wolfrom, available from C&T Publishing, a useful resource to help me work with color effectively.

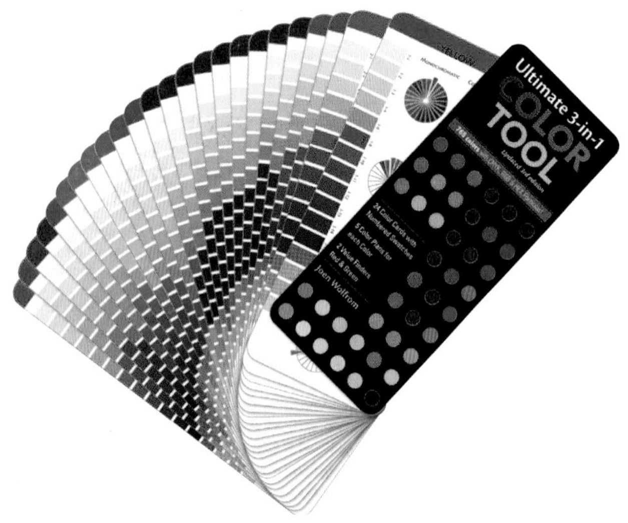

Ultimate 3-in-1 Color Tool

In this book, I am not going to give you a lengthy color lesson because I know you just want to get started making quilts! However, following are a few color basics you might like to know.

The color wheel

The color wheel is a visual representation of colors arranged according to their relationship. Various types of color wheels have been developed over the years, but the one I usually use is divided into twelve segments.

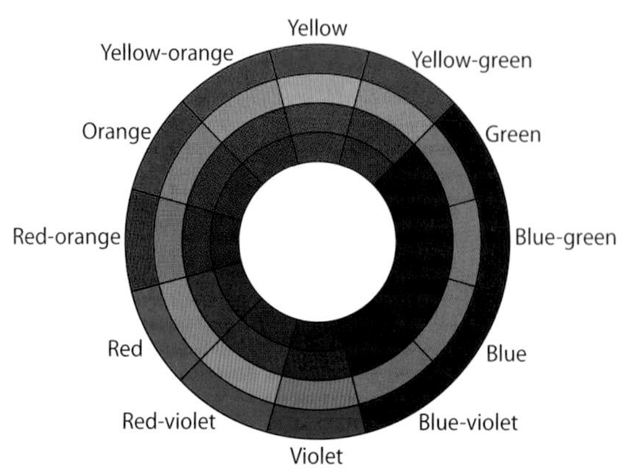

Primary colors

Red, yellow, and blue are the three primary colors that form the basis of all colors we see. They are colors at their most basic and cannot be created by mixing other colors. As a fabric dyer, I create the majority of my colors using a combination of primary colors only. For dyeing purposes, the primary colors are magenta, yellow, and turquoise.

These hand-dyed sets of a twelve-step rainbow were created using two different sets of primaries—warm and cool. Warm colors are usually rich, subtle, and mellow colors, while cool colors are vibrant and have more zing. Generally, we may think of reds and yellows as warm and blues as cool, but there are warm and cool versions of each color. For example, most yellows appear warm next to most blues, but one yellow relative to another yellow could appear cool.

Warm color palette

Cool color palette

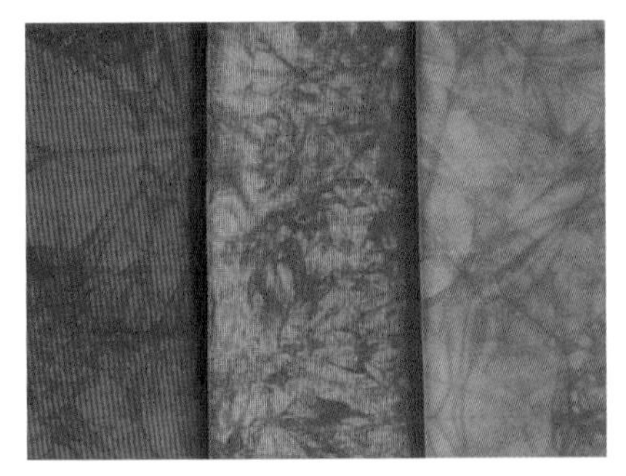
The fabric dyer's cool primary colors are magenta, yellow, and turquoise.

Secondary colors

When two primary colors are mixed together, they form a secondary color. Yellow and red make orange; blue and red make purple; blue and yellow make green.

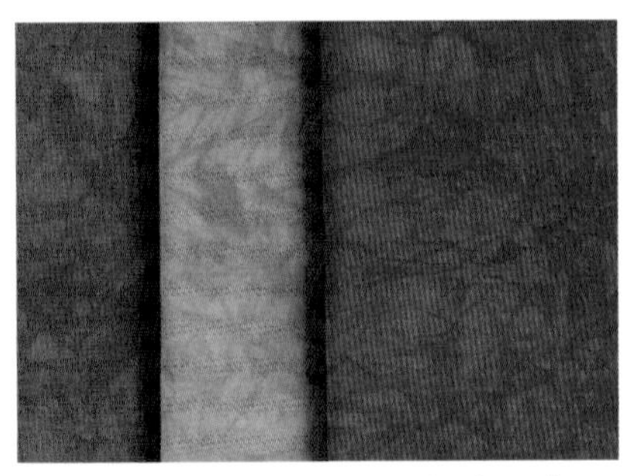
Secondary colors from the cool color palette

Tertiary colors

On the color wheel, tertiary colors lie between a primary and a secondary color and are an equal mix of the two. For example, red-orange is a tertiary color that lies between red and orange.

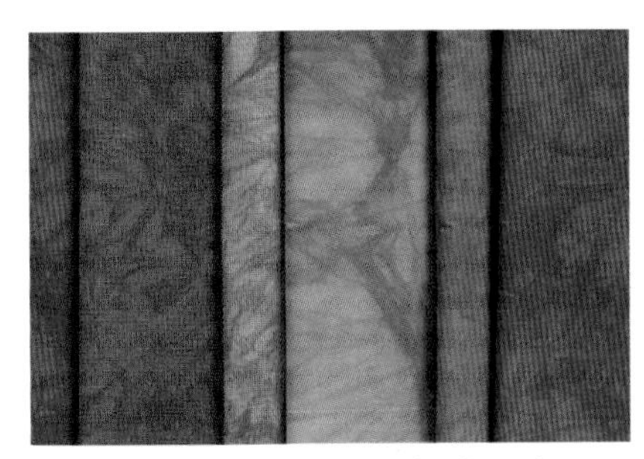
Tertiary color from the cool color palette

Color schemes

Every quilt designer has her or his own personal palette, or preferred color scheme. My preferences are saturated, or intense, colors. I don't work a lot in pastels, and I love quilts that zing.

Monochromatic

A monochromatic color scheme uses just one color, which is lightened by adding white (a tint) or darkened by adding black (a shade). Monochromatic color schemes result in quilts that are peaceful and relaxing to look at.

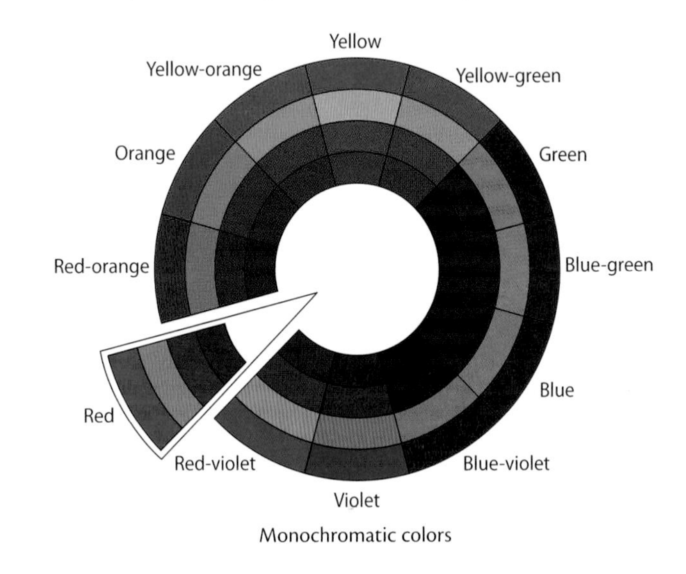

Monochromatic colors

Analogous

Analogous colors are those that lie next to each other on the color wheel, sharing a common hue such as blue. Any three colors make an analogous color scheme, but you can include about five or six colors, and shades and tints of these colors. This color scheme can create a restful look in a quilt.

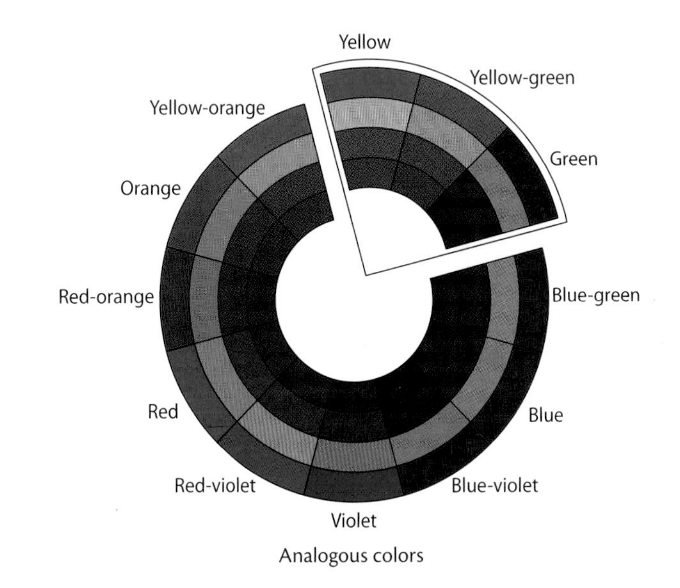

Analogous colors

Complementary

Complementary colors are those opposite each other on the color wheel. Combinations such as purple and yellow or blue and orange create very vibrant and exciting schemes. They do not have to be in equal quantities; a little touch of a complementary color will really add punch to your quilt.

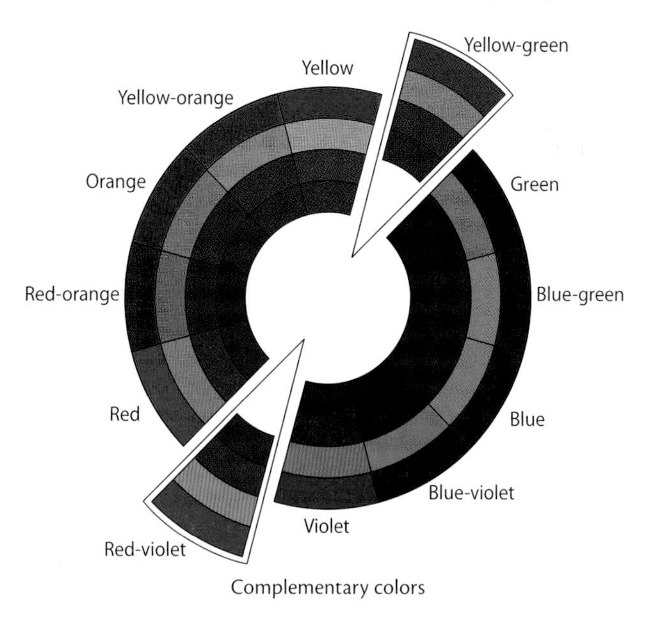

Complementary colors

Partytime, 54″ × 78″, pieced and quilted by Lisa Walton, 2010

Split complementary

One of my favorite color schemes is the split complementary scheme. It is created by selecting a group of analogous colors on the color wheel and then adding the complementary color of the middle one. It always works.

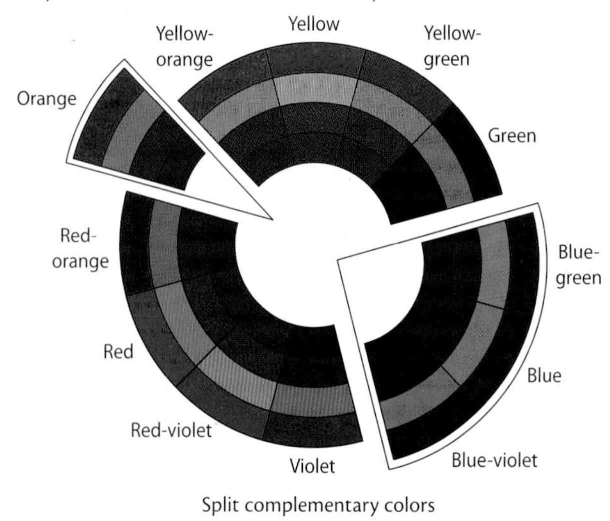

Split complementary colors

Look at how the red-orange really pops in this quilt.

Poor value distribution (left); effective value distribution (right)

Value

Value is basically the degree of lightness or darkness of a color. Using a variety of values in a quilt creates contrast, and thus more interest, even with a monochromatic color scheme.

The choice of fabrics in *Coco Chocolat* (page 26) is a great exercise in using color values, because it was made with 23 fat quarters that were nearly equally divided among light, medium, and dark values. Although some of the colors were mixed throughout the quilt, there is a definite gradation of values from top to bottom. However, as the two illustrations above demonstrate, if *all* the lights, *all* the mediums, and *all* the darks had been placed together, the quilt would have been flatter and less interesting. Including lighter values among the dark values and dark values among the light values creates a continuity of design throughout.

Quilts with high contrast have a dramatic effect, while low contrast gives a quilt a smooth, mellow feel.

When you are laying out your quilt, always check the colors before you sew blocks together to ensure that the values of the quilt blocks produce a pleasing, balanced effect.

Following are some easy ways to check out the design based on color value:

Squint. Squinting makes the eyelashes filter the light coming into our eyes; consequently, light, dark, and medium values appear somewhat more clearly than colors.

Peep. Looking through a camera viewfinder or a door peephole creates a reducing effect that accentuates the values rather than the colors.

Dim. Looking at color in dim light makes the lighter values more pronounced.

Fabric Selection

One of the joys of quilting is choosing fabric. We spend hours fondling it, planning and laying it out, and adding and removing choices. We have our favorite designers or styles or colors.

The quilts in this book are made mainly from hand-dyes or solids. I have chosen to concentrate on the shapes and colors of the blocks rather than on fussy designs. I prefer the clarity and sharpness of solids and the subtle variations and textures of hand-dyed fabric.

I primarily work in my own Dyed & Gone to Heaven hand-dyed fabrics. In addition to dyeing fabric such as the fabric sets shown on page 10, I also enjoy painting fabrics with dyes to create one-of-a kind pieces that can't be easily replicated. If you are interested in hand-dyed fabric, see the information about suppliers of dyes and hand-dyed fabrics in Resources (page 79).

Hand-dyed rainbow

Batiks—especially those with directional patterns such as stripes—also work well with the quilt designs in this book. Good batiks are made using a process that creates somewhat random designs, which work well with the quilt designs.

Fabric used in *Any Which Way* (full quilt on page 53)

I also love working in solids. There is a geometric balance when working with simple shapes and solid colors. The designs are crisp, sharp, and pleasing. I recommend using the lovely and easily available sets of coordinating Kona Cotton Solids fat quarters. These are great when you are not confident in making color selections.

Friendly Geese (full quilt on page 37) was made using a fat quarter bundle of Kona Cotton Solids in the Denim colorstory.

Of course you can use whatever you like, but be aware that highly patterned fabrics may reduce the impact of your designs.

I find that after I have selected my fabrics and they go together the way I like them, then the quilt will work. There could be a single multicolored hand-dyed fabric or 23 fat quarters from a range of solids—but I feel confident that I can put them together in whichever way I finally choose, and they will create an original and pleasing quilt.

In my quilts I use both yardage and scraps from my stash. Quilts made with multiples are perfect for using bits and pieces of your favorite fabrics, because they allow so much flexibility in cutting and piecing.

Designing Your Quilt

After you have designed your basic blocks, you're ready to think about how they will all go together. First, decide the following two things:

1. How big is my quilt going to be? Is it a bed quilt, a lap quilt, or a wallhanging?
2. What fabric will I use? Shall I use that gorgeous piece of hand-dyed fabric that I have been saving for something special, or am I going to raid my stash for as many blues and greens as I can find? Or maybe I'll go to the fabric store after I design the quilt!

Graph-paper sketch of *Any Which Way* (page 53)

Planning Your Quilt

How you plan the quilt depends on which of two types of quilter you are. One is the careful planner, and the other is the serendipitous quilter. I must admit that I am the latter. I usually fly by the seat of my pants and hope it all works out in the end. And if it doesn't—well, I enjoyed the journey!

The careful planner

Using graph paper or a computer program is important if you need to have a firm idea of where you are going before you start cutting and sewing.

Sketch out your plan roughly on graph paper. You don't have to be too exact; just block out areas based on the block design and combinations that you are planning.

If you need to know precise details such as how much fabric you need, or you want to create a cutting diagram, you can draw the design on a computer program such as Electric Quilt.

The Custom Set option in Electric Quilt is perfect for designing a quilt with a random placement of different sizes of the same block. It is very helpful in making design decisions because you can see how modifying color or block placement can completely change the look of your quilt.

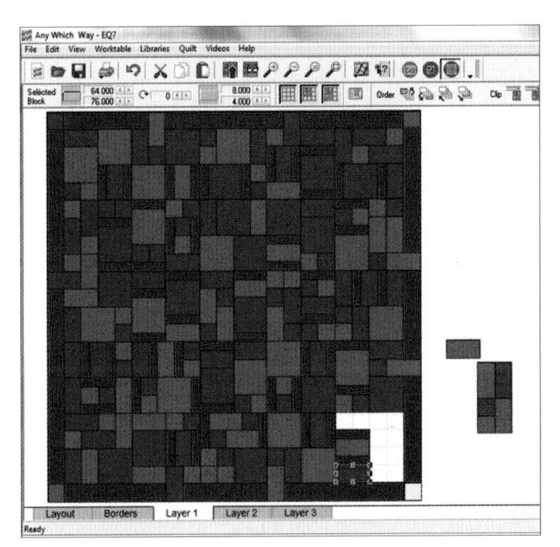

Screen shot of a design in Electric Quilt in Custom Set design mode

The serendipitous quilter

I am the kind of quilter who doesn't plan closely. I usually change my mind many times during the process of creating a quilt. I would really encourage you to try working this way. It is wonderful to play with shapes and colors, and see where they take you.

A design wall is really useful with this style of quilting. You don't need anything fancy—just a large piece of batting or flannel or an inexpensive plastic tablecloth with flannel backing tacked onto a wall will do.

My own design wall is made of a large piece of soft fiberboard covered with extra-wide flannel that is simply pinned on.

A snapshot of my design wall

I usually just start making blocks and placing them randomly on my design wall to see what happens. I experiment until I am happy with my layout.

Calculating Yardage

How much fabric do you need?

Because most of my quilts are designed and made without too much planning, I have worked out rough estimates of the amount of fabric needed. These amounts take into account borders and binding, because there is usually a need to cut these first. See Borders as Design Elements (page 19).

Following are my fabric quantity estimates for three quilt sizes. These estimates don't include backing fabric, and they are based on fabric that is 41″–44″ wide. Amounts can vary depending on your design, the number of pieces your quilt has (many or few pieces), and the number of seams (a lot of fabric is used up in the seam allowances). These estimates and the fabric estimates in the projects may appear generous, but you'll need flexibility for color placement and improvisational design. Keep in mind that design elements such as stripes can affect fabric amounts.

Wallhanging
(18″–24″ × 36″–45″)
4 yards total, which includes 1 yard total for border and binding

Twin bed quilt
(63″–81″ × 87″–106″)
6 yards total, including 1½ yards total for border and binding

Queen bed quilt
(84″–102″ × 92″–111″)
9 yards total, including 2 yards total for border and binding

Cutting the Fabric

Sometimes you have to be very creative with how you cut your fabric. For example, if I am working with a limited amount of fabric such as a hand-dyed fabric, I cut the borders and binding first and put them aside. This way I know that everything that's left can be used in the quilt.

A specific example is *Round the Corner Wallhanging* (page 57). I used a piece of fabric that I had hand painted with dye in gradations from green to orange. I wanted the border fabric to be horizontal, starting in the yellow section, so I cut the borders first. I also wanted to have the orange as the zinger fabric, so I cut a few strips of it next. I then cut the remaining fabric into the simple squares and rectangles required.

Hand-painted fabric for *Round the Corner Wallhanging* (page 57)

Some commercial fabrics have strong directional lines, and it is useful to take these into consideration when cutting. You can use these directional lines as a major feature of your block design, as I did in *Wobbling Windows* (page 61).

Block from *Wobbling Windows*

Creating Modules

Modules are collections of blocks joined together to make a larger section.

Six modules

This is where experimentation comes in. I *always* make up a few blocks in all the sizes first. Sometimes designs look great on paper but just don't translate well to fabric. After all, wouldn't you rather waste some scrap fabric and a little time instead of the precious fabric purchased especially for this quilt?

It is important to make a few blocks to experiment with so that you can see that your blocks work together and can make sure you haven't made any mistakes with the calculations. This step also will allow you to see whether the proportions work or whether you might need to add blocks or change sizes. For instance, do you really want to have to make hundreds of 2″ blocks for a queen-size quilt? Maybe you need to rethink the sizes of your blocks.

All of the designs in this book are made up of various strips of fabric, so I cut a few strips across the width of the fabric and make up the blocks.

As you combine blocks into modules, it is sometimes useful to make up modules of the same length or width, which allows them to be joined together. Also, if you are working with simple shapes that you can put together easily, it is a good idea to decide on a larger module size.

For example, for *Any Which Way* (page 53) I decided to make 8″ × 16″ units and then add them together to form a 16″ × 16″ block.

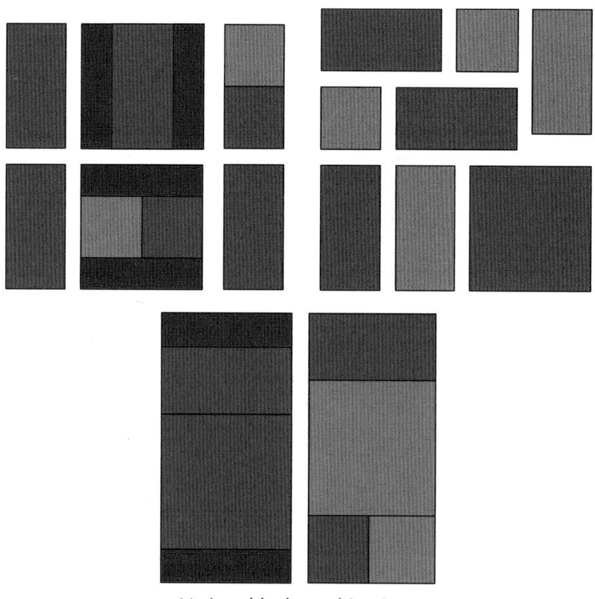

Various block combinations

Small square blocks inserted into gaps for *Slashed* (page 66)

Note

If you run out of fabric or have made too many blocks one size and they should be another, don't worry! Just change the design. Working with limited fabrics or colors should be a fun exercise, and it doesn't matter if it is not perfect. Sometimes these challenges make for a more interesting and unique quilt.

In *Slashed* (page 66) I was working with a limited amount of fabric and just cutting and stitching blocks as they came. When I was laying out the quilt, I realized that none of my blocks fit the gaps I had left. So I just cut up some other ones and fit them to size. Remember—it's your quilt, and you can do whatever you want with it!

Increasing Quilt Size

If you want to make one of the quilts in this book (or any quilt) larger, the modular structure makes it very easy.

The process for adjusting quilt size is different for structured and unstructured quilts. I think of a structured quilt as one with a definite and obvious block pattern structure, such as *Power of Three* (page 22) or *Cornerstones* (page 48). An unstructured quilt is one like *Slashed* (page 66); I don't really know what is going to happen when I take one or two pieces of interesting fabrics and just start cutting.

Structured quilts

Atlantis (page 44) measures 54″ × 78″. It is made up of 6″ and 12″ blocks, in four sets of large and small blocks arranged in columns.

To increase the quilt width by 12″, for example, you would need to make an extra column of blocks—three large blocks and twelve small blocks. This would increase the final size of the quilt to 66″ × 78″.

To increase the quilt width by an additional 12″ (a total of 24″ larger), you would need to make another 12″ column of blocks. One way to do this would be by using two large blocks and sixteen small blocks. This would increase the final size to 78″ × 78″.

You would need to add corresponding border and binding fabric, and amounts can be calculated by adding the widths of the additional blocks.

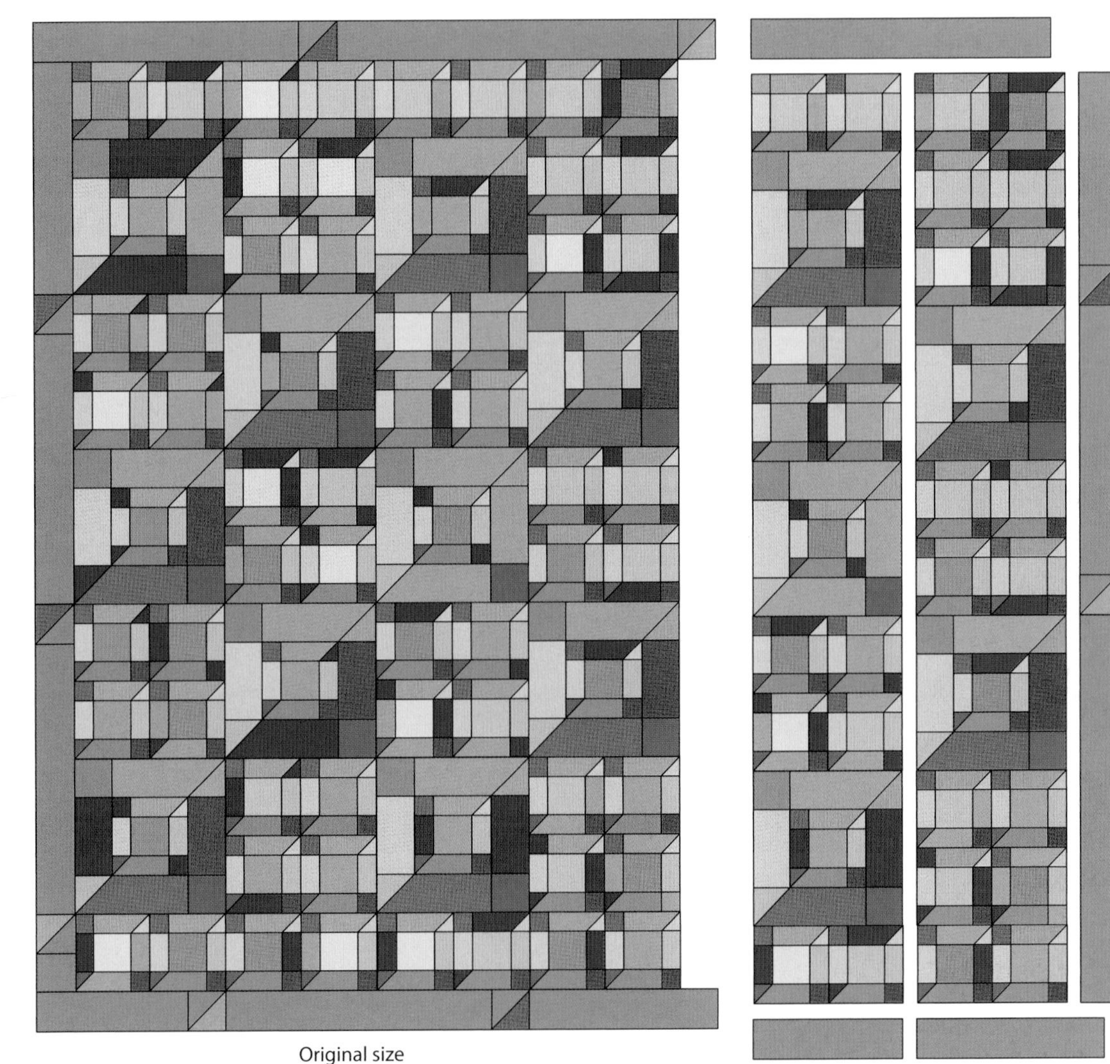

Increasing the width of *Atlantis* by 12″ or 24″

How much extra fabric do you need?

The easiest way to work out how much extra fabric you will need is to work out the proportion of the original quilt.

With *Atlantis*, the original quilt uses approximately 7¼ yards of seven different fabrics. The original design has four columns of blocks, and each one uses approximately ¼ of the total fabric required—approximately 1¾ yards. So two more columns will require approximately 3¾ yards more fabric. This could easily be done by adding an extra ¼ yard to each of the original fabrics or by using some additional coordinating colors for a total of 3¾ yards.

Scrap quilts

If your quilt is basically a scrap quilt, you can calculate the proportion by which you want to increase the size of the quilt and work out the amount of fabric required as for a structured quilt. Then simply add more scraps or increase the quantities of some of the fabrics.

Don't forget to include extra border fabric when making your quilt larger.

Borders as Design Elements

Most of the quilts in this book have blocks extending into the borders. This technique creates an interesting design element and adds to the unique look of the quilt. The method has practical benefits too: You do not need long lengths of fabrics for the borders. Also, breaking up long border strips with blocks creates a stability of structure that helps to reduce ripples in the borders.

When you choose a block to extend into the border, do not add just a small single square, because it will look like it has been put there randomly. Rectangles or larger blocks that extend from the body of the quilt into the border work best.

Also, when laying out your quilt top, try not to place the extended block directly opposite one on the other side, because this creates a division in your quilt that can look a little odd.

Block extending into the border in *Coco Chocolat* (full quilt on page 26)

Method

As you design your quilt, select one of the blocks that you would like to extend into the border. In this example the blocks are 2″ and 4″ squares and rectangles, and the 2″ × 4″ rectangle will extend into the border.

Rectangles that will extend into the border area

The border fabric is always cut to the width of one of the smaller blocks. In this example the border is cut to 2½″ wide, so the finished border will be 2″—the size of the small square.

Add your chosen extending block as follows:

1. Stitch the extending block to the adjacent blocks. Stop stitching at least 1″ from the edge; these last few inches will be stitched after you attach the border.

Stitch, stopping at least 1″ from edge.

2. On the top edge of the quilt, measure the distance between the side of the quilt and the first extending block, and add ½″ for the seam allowances. Cut the border strip to that length.

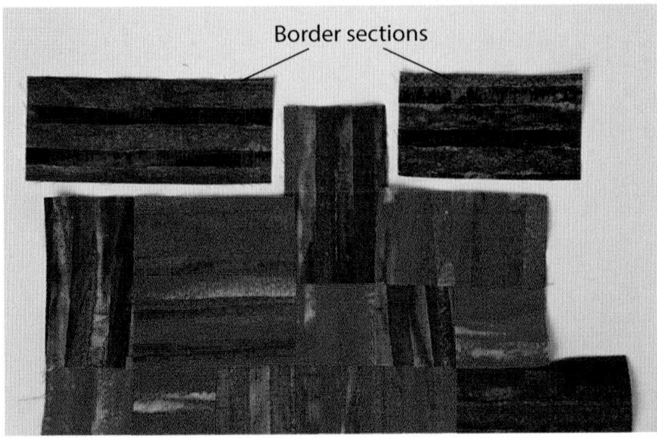

Measure and cut border sections.

3. Pin the border in place on the quilt top, and repeat on the other side of the extended block. Stitch the border sections to the quilt top.

Stitch border sections to quilt top.

4. Press the seam allowances toward the border, fold the border down, away from the quilt top, and press.

Border sections pressed into place

5. Repeat for all border pieces on the top and bottom of the quilt.

6. Now fold the quilt top so that the edges of the extending block and the border piece are aligned right sides together, and stitch from the original stopping point to the edge of the quilt.

Stitch remaining section of seam to edge of quilt.

7. Repeat the process for the sides of the quilt, incorporating the border length as well.

Finished borders

Power of Three

Finished block sizes: 9″ × 9″, 6″ × 6″, 3″ × 3″
Finished quilt size: 69″ × 72″

This quilt started off as a beginner's lesson in making a simple Four-Patch, and then it grew and grew. It is a perfect quilt for using up scraps of all sizes in your favorite colors. I used my own hand-dyed fabrics, which have subtle color variations. It also would look wonderful in batiks. It features the Four-Patch with block borders made in three sizes.

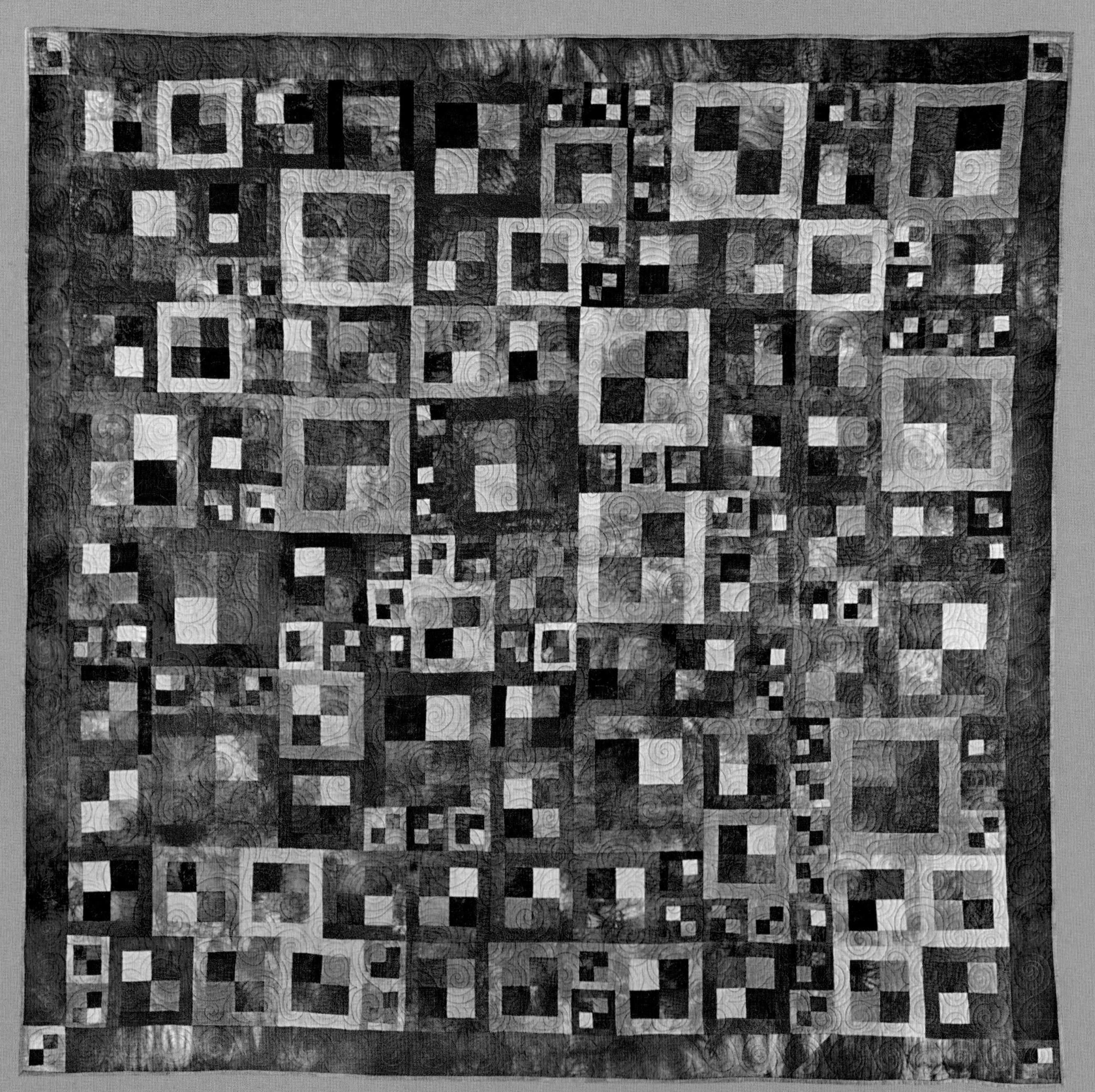

Designed and pieced by Lisa Walton, and quilted by Nic Bridges, 2003

Fabric Requirements

Yardages are based on 44″-wide fabric. All seams allowances are a scant ¼″.

5¼ yards of hand dyes, batiks, or solid scraps in coordinating colors for the blocks

1 yard of red fabric for the border

⅝ yard of chartreuse fabric for the binding

4½ yards or a 75″ × 78″ piece for the backing (I used one of the fabrics in the quilt.)

75″ × 78″ batting

Cutting

WOF = width of fabric

From the assorted scraps:

LARGE BLOCKS:

Cut 4 squares 3½ ″ × 3½″ per large block for 17 blocks—total 68 squares.

Cut 2 strips 2″ × 6½″ and 2 strips 2″ × 9½″ for the block borders—total 34 strips of each size.

MEDIUM BLOCKS:

Cut 4 squares 2½″ × 2½″ per medium block for 60 blocks—total 240 squares.

Cut 2 strips 1½″ × 4½″ and 2 strips 1½″ × 6½″ for the block borders—total 120 strips of each size.

SMALL BLOCKS:

Cut 4 squares 1½″ × 1½″ per small block for 73 blocks—total 292 squares.

Cut 2 strips 1″ × 2½″ and 2 strips 1″ × 3½″ for the block borders—total 146 strips of each size.

From the red fabric:

Cut 7 strips 3½″ × WOF.

From the chartreuse fabric:

Cut 7 strips 2¼″ × WOF.

Tip

The cutting instructions are only a starting point for creating the blocks. This is a scrap quilt, so each block can contain a variety of fabrics in the squares and strips. I suggest making a few large blocks first. I like to start by making the large 9″ × 9″ blocks with larger pieces of fabric; as the pieces get smaller, so do the blocks.

BLOCKS

1. Lay out 4 squares of the same size, choosing squares of varying colors or values to create contrast. Sew the squares together in pairs, and then sew the pairs together, with seams pressed in opposite directions.
2. Stitch the short border strips to the left and right of the Four-Patch block. Press seams toward the borders.
3. Stitch the long border strips to the top and bottom of the Four-Patch block. Press seams toward the borders.

Make 17 large blocks, 60 medium blocks, and 73 small blocks.

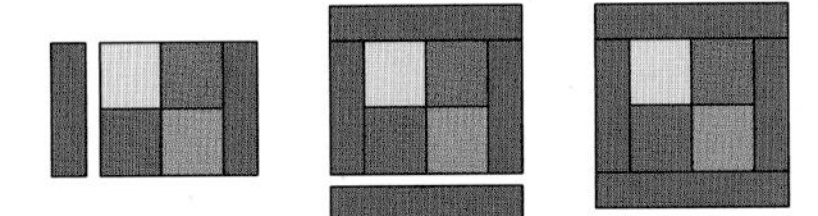

Piece the Four-Patch blocks.

Tip

If you have yardage or large scraps for the squares of the Four-Patch blocks, you could save time by joining fabric strips and then cross-cutting to make pairs. Large blocks would require 3½″ strips; medium, 2½″; and small, 1½″.

QUILT TOP

1. Set aside 4 small blocks for the border corners.

2. Referring to the assembly diagram or creating your own design, build the blocks into modules that have the same length (or width) so that they can be sewn together. A medium block will match 2 small blocks sewn together; a large block will match 3 small blocks or a medium and a small block.

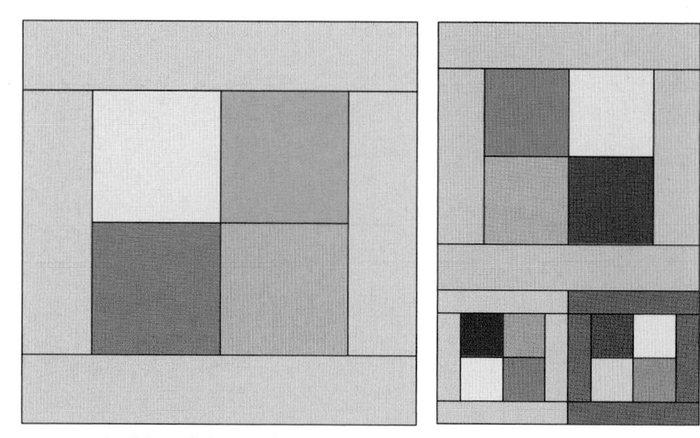

Build modules combining small, medium, and large blocks.

3. When you have an arrangement you like, sew the modules together to form rows or partial rows. Continue to sew the modules together to form the quilt top.

Borders

1. Sew together the cut border strips to create a long strip.

2. To calculate the top and bottom border length, add the individual block sizes across the quilt top. The top (and bottom) measurement is 66″. Adding ½″ for the ¼″ seam allowances brings the total to 66½″.

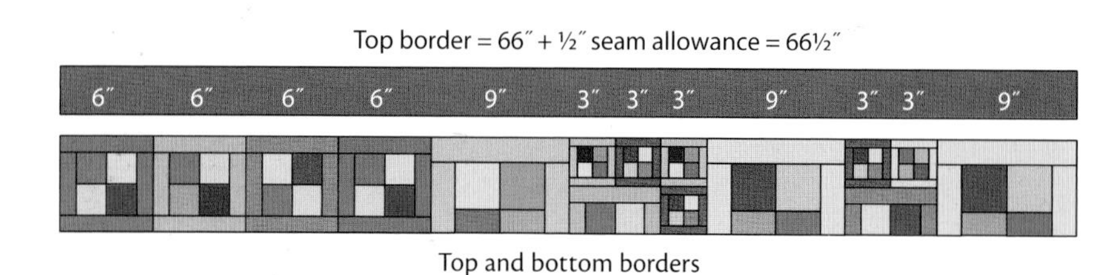

Top and bottom borders

3. Cut 2 pieces 66½″.

4. Then calculate the side borders. Add the block sizes, which total 63″; then add ½″ for the ¼″ seam allowances, bringing the total to 63½″.

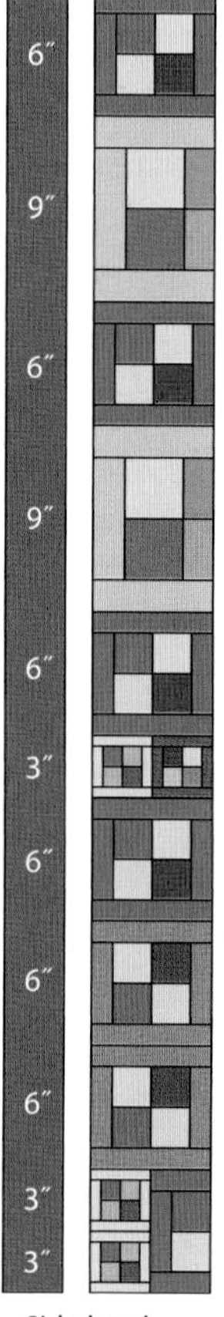

Side borders

5. Divide the quilt top into quarters and mark each midpoint with a pin. Fold the border strips to find and mark each center. Pin a 66½″ strip to the top, matching marks, and stitch together. Repeat for the bottom border. Press seams toward the borders.

6. Using the 4 small blocks that were set aside, stitch a block to each end of the side borders.

7. Matching center marks, pin and stitch side borders into place.

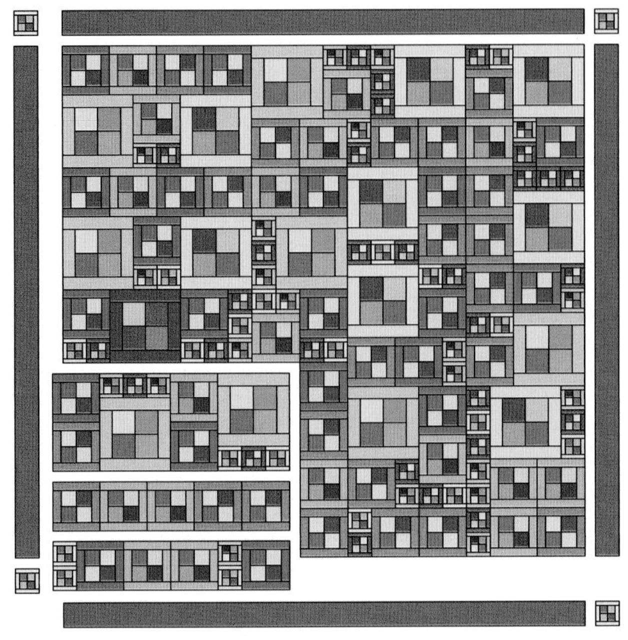

Assembly diagram

FINISHING

1. Refer to Quiltmaking Basics (page 74) to layer and baste your quilt to prepare it for quilting.
2. Quilt as desired. This project was quilted on a longarm machine in a spiral pattern using variegated thread. The quilting creates a pleasing balance for the angles through an organic circular pattern.
3. Refer to Quiltmaking Basics to bind and finish your quilt.

Bonus Project:

Coco Chocolat

Finished block sizes: 9″ × 9″, 6″ × 6″, 3″ × 3″

Finished quilt size: 60″ × 78″

This quilt uses the same block sizes as *Power of Three* (page 22) but interprets the design in a very different color palette that includes rich browns reminiscent of chocolate, so it is named accordingly. This monochromatic quilt was made using a bundle of 23 solid fat quarters with nearly equal amounts of light, medium, and dark values, affording a perfect opportunity to create an effective distribution of values. Some blocks extend into the borders as an integral part of this quilt design.

Designed by Lisa Walton, pieced by Maggie Gilbert, and quilted by Kimpossible Quilting, 2012

Fabric Requirements

Yardages are based on 44″-wide fabric.

23 fat quarters in monochromatic solids with equal amounts of light, medium, and dark values for the blocks*

1 yard for the border*

⅝ yard for the binding*

3¾ yards or a 66″ × 84″ piece for the backing

66″ × 84″ piece of batting

** I used a fat quarter bundle of Kona Cotton Solids in the Grounded colorstory, plus additional fat quarters of two colors in the set: Nutmeg for the border and Brown for the binding.*

Cutting

WOF = width of fabric

From the border fabric:*

Cut 6 strips 3½″ × WOF.

From the binding fabric:*

Cut 8 strips 2¼″ × WOF.

** Remaining border and binding fabric can be used in the blocks.*

BLOCKS

Coco Chocolat contains 20 large blocks, 48 medium blocks, and 72 small blocks. Your block counts will vary if you designed your own layout.

1. Divide the fat quarters evenly into 3 groups—2 groups of 8 and a group of 7—each with similar amounts of light, medium, and dark fabrics. You will cut the pieces for the blocks as you did the scraps in *Power of Three* (Cutting, page 23).

Tip

Don't make all your blocks at once. Make the large blocks from the first pile of fat quarters, and then make some medium and small blocks from the remaining piles. Start laying out your quilt, and then use all the remaining fabric randomly to make medium and small blocks as required to complete the quilt top. If you make all your blocks before laying out your quilt, you may not have enough of the required shapes to fill the gaps.

2. From a group of 8 fat quarters, cut the large 9″ × 9″ block pieces. For each block, cut 4 squares 3½″ × 3½″ (80 total), 2 rectangles 2″ × 6½″ (40 total), and 2 rectangles 2″ × 9½″ (40 total). Cut pieces for as many large blocks as you can.

3. From the second group of 8 fat quarters, cut the medium 6″ × 6″ block pieces. For each block cut 4 squares 2½″ × 2½″ (192 total), 2 rectangles 1½″ × 4½″ (96 total), and 2 rectangles 1½″ × 6½″ (96 total). Cut pieces for about 20 medium blocks.

4. From the group of 7 fat quarters, cut the small 3″ × 3″ block pieces. For each block, cut 4 squares 1½″ × 1½″ (288 total), 2 rectangles 1″ × 2½″ (144 total), and 2 rectangles 1″ × 3½″ (144 total). Cut pieces for about 40 small blocks.

5. Make the blocks, following Steps 1–3 in Blocks for *Power of Three* (page 23).

QUILT TOP

1. Start laying out the quilt top, and then use the remaining fabric to make small and medium blocks to fill the gaps.

2. Referring to the assembly diagram (page 29) or creating your own design, lay out the completed blocks. Build modules: A medium block will match 2 small blocks sewn together; a large block will match 3 small blocks or a medium and a small block.

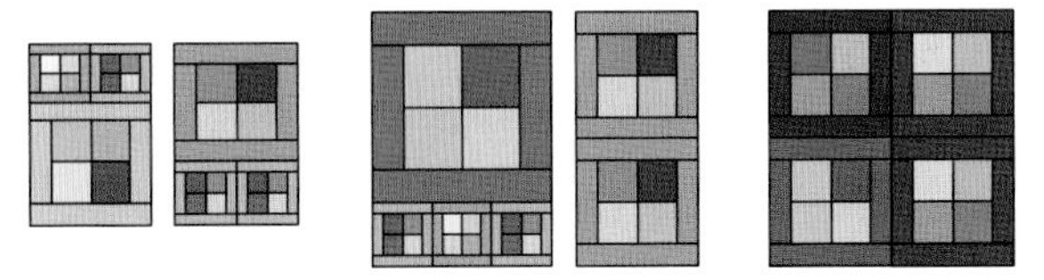

Some module layout suggestions

Tip

Stitch the blocks into modules of the same size (either length or width) so it is easier to piece them together.

3. To make the design more interesting, place a large block on each side extending 3″ into the border, as shown in the assembly diagram. (For instructions, refer to Borders as Design Elements, page 19.)

4. When you have an arrangement of blocks that you like, sew the blocks or modules together to form the quilt top.

Borders

1. Sew the 6 strips of 3½″ border fabric into a long strip.

2. Measure the length needed for each border section. To do this, add the finished sizes of all the blocks in a section and then add ½″ for the 2 seam allowances, as in Borders for *Power of Three* (page 24). For example, the border strips in *Coco Chocolat* have the following sizes:
12½″, 18½″ (cut 2), 21½″, 33½″, 36½″, 42½″, 45½″.

Tip

These measurements are for the quilt layout used in *Coco Chocolat*, so if your layout is different, measure to find the length of the border strips. As you add the final border strips, remember to account for the width of the previously added border (3″ at each corner).

3. Following the instructions in Borders as Design Elements (page 19), pin and stitch the borders to the quilt.

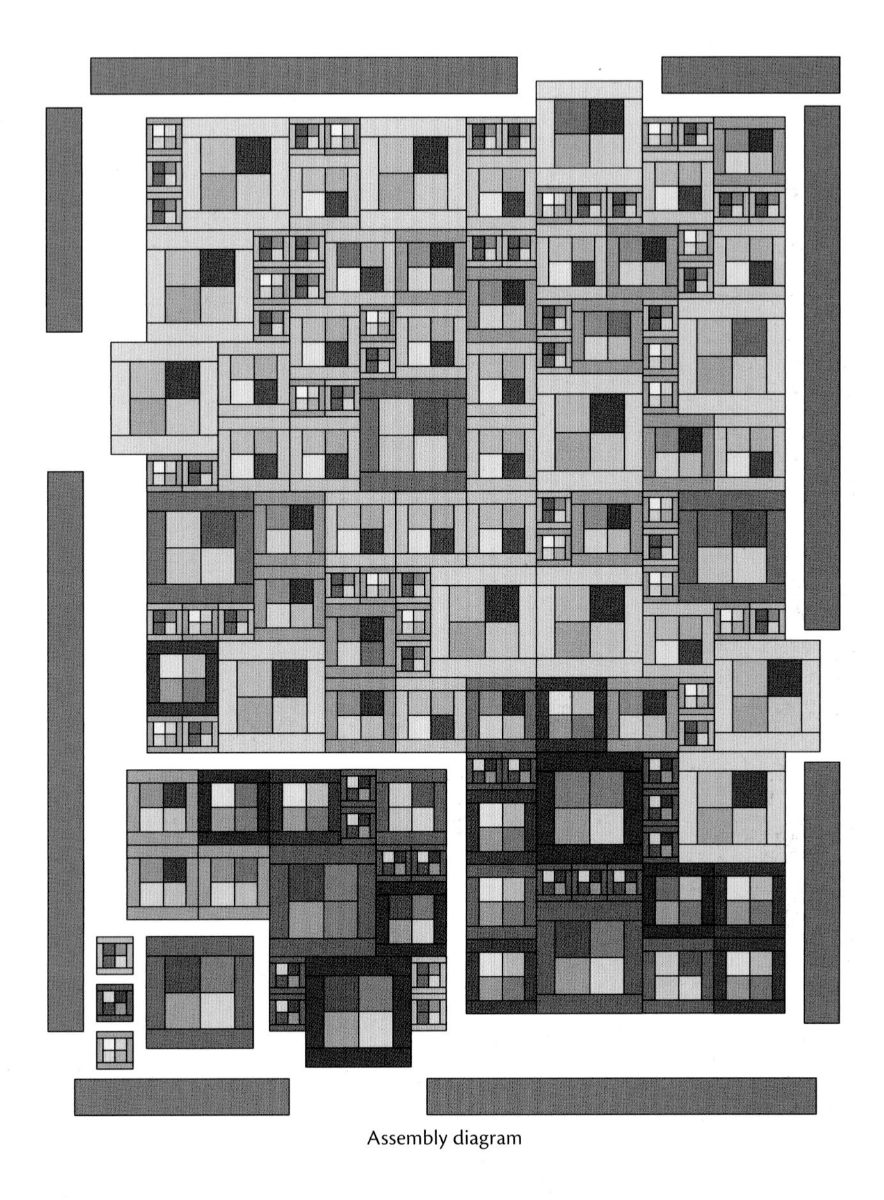

Assembly diagram

FINISHING

1. Refer to Quiltmaking Basics (page 74) to layer and baste your quilt to prepare it for quilting.

2. Quilt as desired. This quilt was quilted on a longarm machine in a square spiral pattern using variegated thread. Another approach would be to stitch horizontally or vertically across each block.

3. Refer to Quiltmaking Basics to bind and finish your quilt.

Dancing Nines

Finished block sizes: 6″ × 6″, 3″ × 3″
Finished quilt size: 60″ × 72″

This quilt uses the very simple Nine-Patch block in just two sizes. An analogous color scheme of blues and greens in a variety of values gives it a harmonious yet interesting look. The quilt is made using a quick method for cutting and making strip sets.

Designed and pieced by Lisa Walton, and machine quilted by Kimpossible Quilting, 2012

Fabric Requirements

Yardages are based on 44″-wide fabric.

25 fat quarters in analogous solid colors for the blocks*

1 yard of solid white for the blocks

4½ yards for the backing and facing

66″ × 78″ piece of batting

** I used a fat quarter bundle of Kona Cotton Solids in the Poseidon colorstory, plus four additional Kona Cotton Solids fat quarters in Tarragon, Green Tea, Zucchini, and Celery. A scrap of Chartreuse was used as a highlight.*

Note

I used a fat quarter set of 21 colors for this quilt. I realized I wanted a few more to make the quilt a more useful size, so I simply added more analogous colors. The white fabric brought lightness to the combination.

If you have fewer fabrics or want less color variation, you need larger quantities of fewer fabrics. For instance, twelve half-yards of analogous colors with a yard of white would yield the same number of blocks and the same size quilt.

Instead of fat quarters, you can also use cut yardage or scraps, as long as you have approximately equal quantities of pairs of fabrics.

Large blocks

1. Choose 2 fat quarters and stack them together. Cut 7 strips 2½″ × width of fabric, to yield 14 strips.

2. Stitch strips together in pairs and then stitch a third strip to make 2 different combinations as shown. You'll use 12 of the 14 strips to make 4 sets of 3 strips. Cut the last 2 strips in half, one of each color, and continue making strip sets.

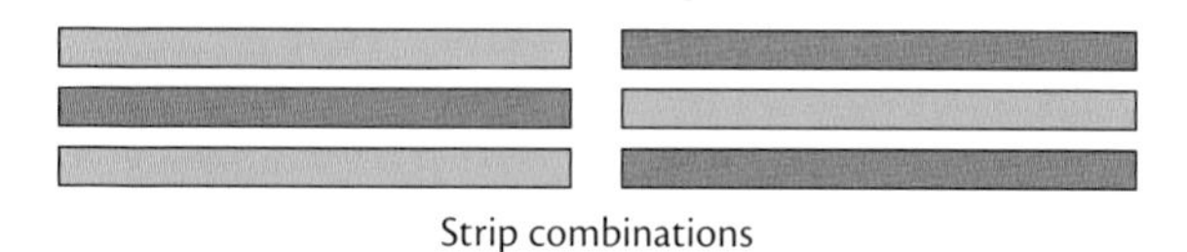

Strip combinations

3. Crosscut the strips into 2½″ strips.

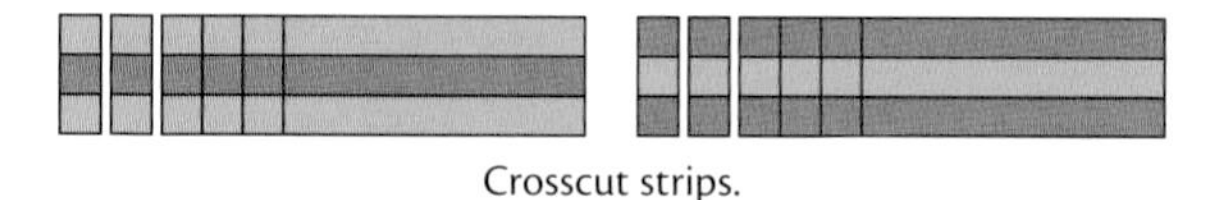

Crosscut strips.

4. Stitch alternate sets together as shown. This method yields 12 large blocks per pair of fat quarters.

Stitch sets together.

BLOCKS

Use strip piecing as described above for the blocks. You will need 60 large blocks and 240 small blocks.

5. Repeat Steps 1–4 with another pair of fat quarters, yielding another 12 large blocks. You can continue until you have 60 large blocks (total of 5 pairs of fat quarters) or, if you prefer, cut as you go, creating even more color combinations.

Small blocks

Using the same technique as for the large blocks:

1. Stack 2 fat quarters, and cut 12 strips 1½″ across the width of the fabric. This technique yields 34 complete small blocks per fat quarter pair. Use white fabric in some combinations to add brightness and contrast.

2. Follow Steps 2–4 of the instructions for the large blocks.

3. Repeat with another pair of fat quarters. You can continue until you have 240 small blocks (7 pairs of fat quarters, plus 2 blocks from scraps) or, if you prefer, cut as you go, creating even more color combinations.

QUILT TOP

1. Follow the assembly diagram to lay out the blocks, or use your own design.

2. Stitch 6 small blocks together in a row; repeat to make a total of 10 rows with 6 blocks each.

3. Stitch 10 rows of blocks together to create the center panel.

Tip

Match and pin all seams together in all rows before sewing to ensure accuracy.

4. Sew 2 sets of 3 large blocks together. Sew a set to the top and a set to the bottom of the center panel.

5. Sew 2 sets of 7 large blocks together. Sew to the sides of the center panel.

6. Stitch 10 small blocks together in a row. Repeat for 6 rows, and join rows to make 2 sets of 3 rows. Stitch them to the top and bottom of the center panel.

7. Stitch 20 small blocks together in a row. Repeat for 6 rows, and join rows to make 2 sets of 3 rows. Stitch them to the sides of the center panel.

8. Stitch 8 large blocks together in a row. Repeat for 2 rows, and stitch these to the top and bottom of the center panel.

9. Stitch 12 large blocks together in a row. Repeat for 2 rows, and stitch these to the sides of the center panel.

Assembly diagram

FINISHING

1. Refer to Quiltmaking Basics (page 74) to layer and baste your quilt to prepare it for quilting.

2. Quilt as desired. This quilt has been quilted on a longarm machine with an allover spiral design to accentuate the feeling of movement.

3. This quilt is finished with a facing rather than a binding. A facing finish creates a sharper edge to the quilt and is a good choice when a quilt would look better without a frame, as does this one. From the 4½ yards of backing and facing fabric, cut 7 strips 2¼″ across the width of fabric. Refer to Quiltmaking Basics to face and finish your quilt.

Bonus Project:

Two Up Wallhanging

Finished block sizes: 6″ × 6″, 3″ × 3″
Finished quilt size: 42″ × 42″

This smaller wallhanging version of *Dancing Nines* (page 30) was made with only two fabrics—orange and purple hand-dyed cotton sateens. I wanted to see how effective two contrasting colors would be. You could also use batiks or solids. I named this quilt *Two Up* in reference to an iconic Australian gambling game in which two pennies are tossed up in the air.

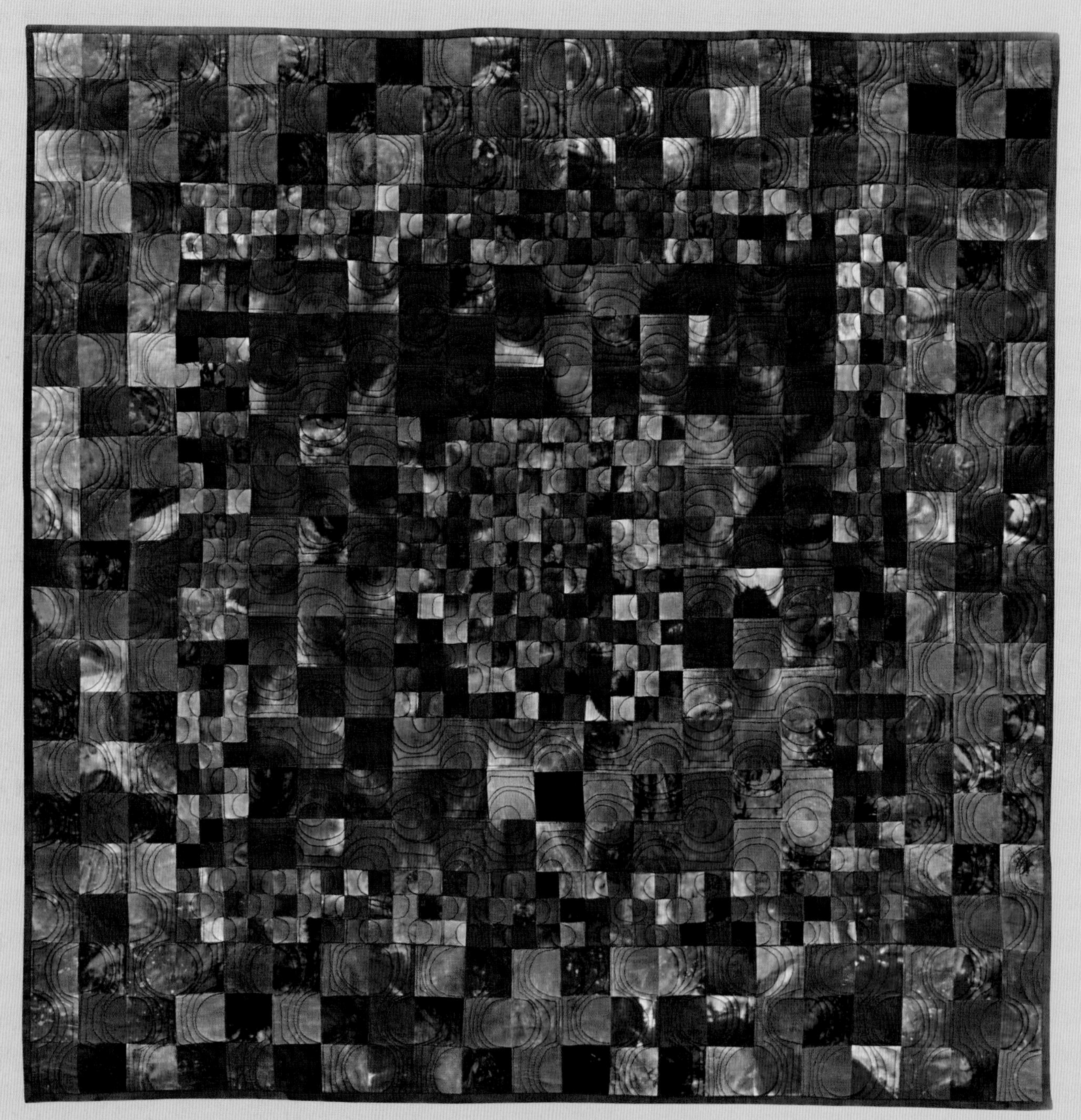

Designed, pieced, and quilted by Lisa Walton, 2011

Fabric Requirements

Yardages are based on 44″-wide fabric.

1½ yards of hand dyes, batiks, or mottled solids in orange, gold, and red for the blocks

1½ yards of hand dyes, batiks, or mottled solids in purple, blue, and violet for the blocks

3 yards for the backing and binding

48″ × 48″ batting

BLOCKS

1. To make the blocks, follow the instructions for *Dancing Nines* (Blocks, page 31). For this version, you will need 36 large blocks and 52 small blocks.
2. To lay out the blocks, refer to the assembly diagram.

QUILT TOP

1. Stitch 4 small blocks together into a row, and repeat for 4 rows, alternating the colors as shown for the center panel. Take care to match seams.
2. Stitch the 4 rows of small blocks together to create the center panel.
3. Stitch 2 large blocks together and stitch them to a side of the center panel. Repeat for the other side, making sure to alternate block colors as shown.
4. Stitch 4 large blocks together, and stitch them to the top of the center panel. Repeat for the bottom, alternating colors.
5. Stitch 8 small blocks together into a row, and stitch them to one side of the center panel. Repeat for the other side, ensuring colors are alternating.
6. Stitch 10 small blocks together, and stitch them to the top of the center panel. Repeat for the bottom.
7. Stitch 5 large blocks together in a row, and stitch them to one side of the center panel. Repeat for the other side, ensuring colors are alternating.
8. Stitch 7 large blocks together and stitch to the top. Repeat for the bottom.

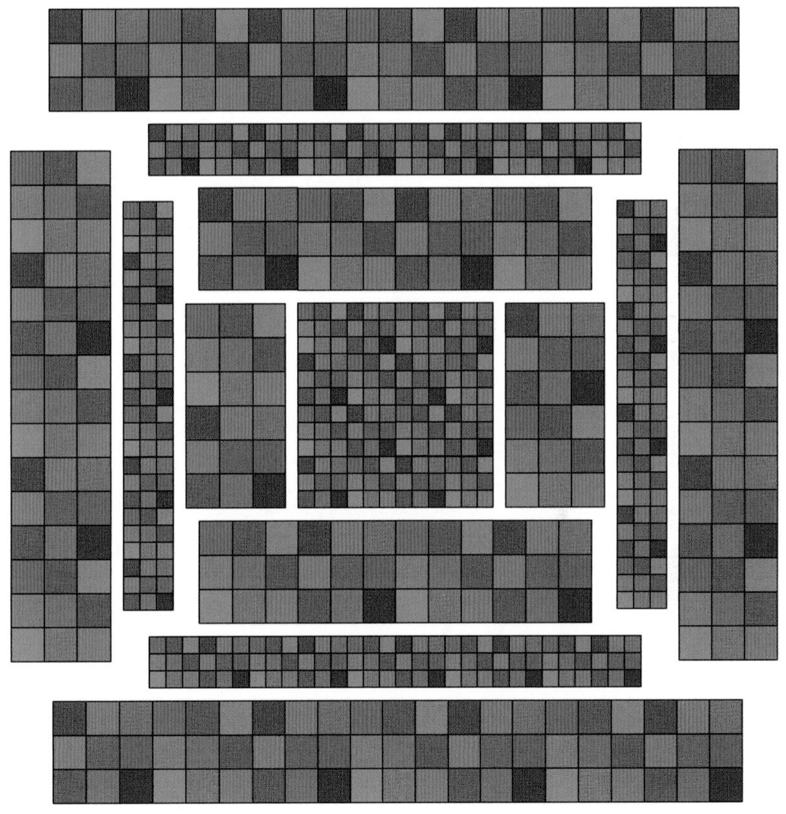

Assembly diagram

FINISHING

1. Refer to Quiltmaking Basics (page 74) to layer and baste your quilt and prepare it for quilting.
2. Quilt as desired. This quilt has been machine quilted in sections with a free-motion bubble design as described in Quilting a Bubble Design.
3. From the backing and binding fabric, cut 4 strips 2¼″ × width of fabric for the binding. Refer to Quiltmaking Basics to bind and finish your quilt.

Quilting a Bubble Design

A bubble quilting design can be used for blocks with many different shapes, including squares, rectangles, stars, and leaves. In this quilt, the center section with small blocks is quilted vertically with smaller bubbles. The large blocks surrounding the center are quilted with the same design, but on a larger scale and horizontally direction. The outer row of small blocks is quilted vertically in the smaller scale.

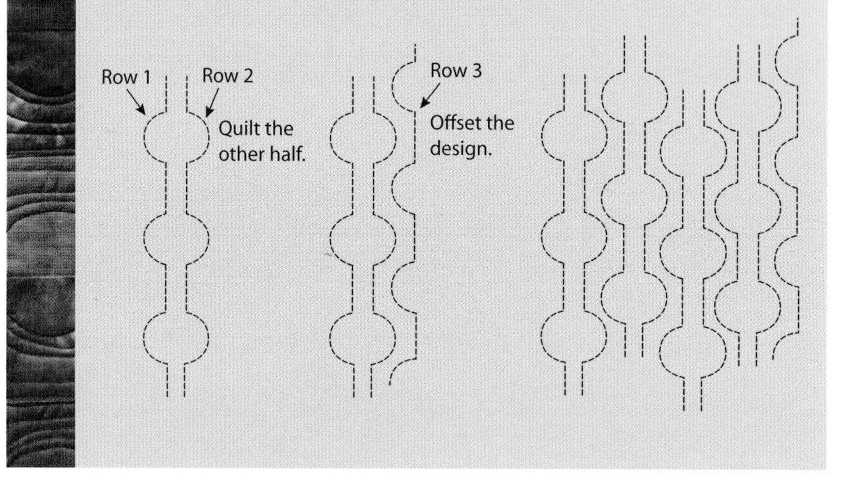

Friendly Geese

Finished block sizes: 8″ × 8″, 4″ × 4″

Finished quilt size: 68″ × 76″

This quilt uses two block sizes of the traditional Flying Geese pattern. Usually the "geese" are flying in the same direction, but not these. They are very friendly but confused, and they keep bumping into each other and flying off in all directions!

In this project you will learn a quick and easy technique for making Flying Geese blocks. This quilt is made using commercial solid fabrics in a monochromatic scheme, using a range of light to dark values to create interesting contrasting effects.

Designed and pieced by Lisa Walton, and machine quilted by Kimpossible Quilting, 2012

Fabric Requirements

Yardages are based on 44″-wide fabric.

22 fat quarters in blue solids in a range of values for the blocks*

1½ yards of a solid for borders and binding*

4¼ yards for the backing*

74″ × 82″ batting

** I used a fat quarter bundle of Kona Cotton Solids in the Denim colorstory. I used additional yardage of two colors from the bundle: Marine for the borders and binding, and Ocean for the backing.*

Tip

This quilt is designed using fat quarters (18″ × 22″), but cut yardage or scraps can be used as long as you have equal quantities of fabric pairs.

BLOCKS

Following is a quick method for making Flying Geese blocks. You will need 44 large blocks and 87 small blocks. For this quilt, 2 Flying Geese units are joined to make a block.

1. Choose 2 fat quarters of contrasting value. Stack together, and cut squares as shown. This technique yields 4 complete large blocks and 8 complete small blocks per fat quarter pair.

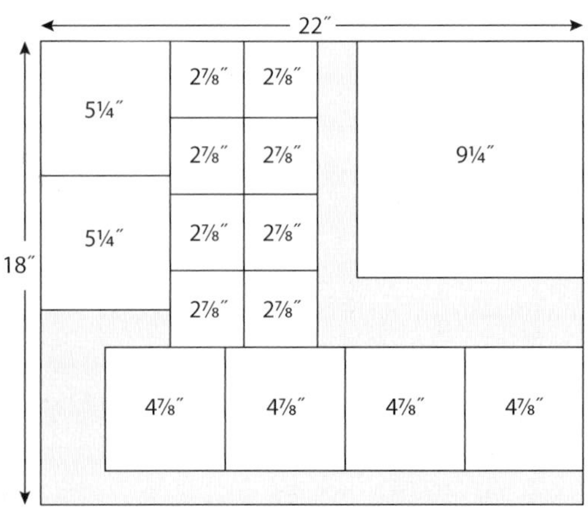

Cutting diagram

Tip

To create the most striking blocks, it is best to have two contrasting values when you pair the fabrics. Try to pair dark fabrics with light and medium for maximum effect. I added a few low-contrast pairs, both dark or both medium, for interest.

2. To make the large Flying Geese blocks, use a 9¼″ square paired with 2 squares 4⅞″ × 4⅞″. For the small Flying Geese blocks, use a 5¼″ square with 2 squares 2⅞″ × 2⅞″. Place 2 small squares on opposite corners of the large square. They will overlap in the middle. Draw a diagonal line with a fabric or chalk marker. Draw lines a scant ¼″ on both sides of the diagonal.

3. Stich along the 2 outside lines, and then cut along the center diagonal. Press the small triangles to the outside.

4. Place a small square on each corner. Mark the diagonal and stitching lines as before.

5. Stitch along the outside lines, and then cut along the center diagonal. Press the triangle to the outside; trim the large geese units to measure 4½″ × 8½″; trim the small units to 2½″ × 4½″.

6. Repeat Steps 1–5 with opposite colors, and then stitch together opposite units as shown to create a block.

QUILT TOP

Refer to the assembly diagram (page 40) or lay out the blocks in your own design. The side of a large block will match 2 small blocks sewn together, and changing the direction of the Flying Geese blocks allows even more design possibilities.

Tip

If you are creating your own layout, you may want to position the larger blocks on a design wall or other work surface first; then fill in gaps with the small blocks. This will help you to balance the color and scale. You can form modules into rows, or keep building up modules and joining them in larger sections, to construct the quilt top.

Borders

This border treatment features four blocks extending into the borders, becoming part of the overall design.

1. From the 1½ yards of border and binding fabric, cut 6 strips 4½″ × width of fabric for the border. Set aside the rest for the binding.

2. If you created your own layout, measure and cut border strips according to your design. If you followed the layout in *Friendly Geese*, cut a border strip in each of the following lengths: 16½″, 20½″, 32½″, 40½″, and 44½″; and cut 3 border strips 28½″ long each.

3. Following the instructions in Borders as Design Elements (page 19), pin and stitch the borders to the quilt.

Assembly diagram

Changing the Block Size

To make the quilt the size in this project, I used eleven pairs of fabrics in fat quarters. You could also change the block size to change the size of the finished quilt. This would mean changing the border width and adjusting the cutting layouts.

To make the Flying Geese units, you need a square that is the width of the finished unit *plus* 1¼″, and 4 squares that are the height of the finished unit *plus* ⅞″.

In this quilt, for the large Flying Geese units to be 4″ × 8″ finished, the squares are 4⅞″ and 9¼″. A pair of these will make a large 8″ × 8″ block.

For small Flying Geese units to be 2″ × 4″ finished, the squares are 2⅞″ and 5¼″. A pair of these will make a small 4″ × 4″ block.

FINISHING

1. Refer to Quiltmaking Basics (page 74) to layer and baste your quilt to prepare it for quilting.
2. Quilt as desired. This quilt has been quilted in an allover swirling design to balance the sharp geometric angles of the diamond shapes.
3. From the remainder of the border and binding fabric, cut 8 strips 2¼″ × width of fabric for the binding. Refer to Quiltmaking Basics to bind and finish your quilt.

Bonus Project:

Peaceful Geese

Finished block sizes: 8″ × 8″, 4″ × 4″

Finished quilt size: 44″ × 60″

The same Flying Geese block in two sizes is used in this smaller version of *Friendly Geese.* The fabrics used in this quilt are a set of my own hand-dyed fabrics in subdued analogous hues of green and gold. Using analogous colors in a quilt creates a peaceful feel. To give the quilt a bit of a zing, I added complementary shades of coral and orange. For additional information, refer to Understanding Color (page 10). Of course, you can feel free to substitute batiks or solids.

Designed and pieced by Lisa Walton, and machine quilted by Kimpossible Quilting, 2012

Fabric Requirements

Yardages are based on 44″-wide fabric.

½ yard each of 5 fabrics in analogous shades of green to gold for the blocks

½ yard in complementary coral to orange for the blocks

1 yard for the borders and binding

2¾ yards or a 50″ × 66″ piece for the backing

50″ × 66″ batting

BLOCKS

To make the blocks, follow the instructions in *Friendly Geese* (Blocks, page 38). For this version, you will need 20 large blocks and 47 small blocks. A block is made by joining 2 Flying Geese units with opposing colors.

QUILT TOP

Refer to the assembly diagram, or lay out the blocks in your own design. You can choose to cluster the blocks that contain complementary colors or distribute them for the desired effect. Sew together 2 small blocks to match a large block, 4 small blocks to form a square of the same size as a large block, and so on.

Borders

This border treatment features 5 large blocks extending into the borders, becoming part of the overall design.

1. From the border and binding fabric, cut 4 strips 4½″ × width of fabric. Set aside the rest for the binding.
2. If you created your own layout, measure and cut border strips according to your design. If you followed the layout in *Peaceful Geese*, cut border strips as follows: a strip 4½″, a strip 12½″, 3 strips 16½″, 2 strips 20½″, and 2 strips 24½″.
3. Following the instructions in Borders as Design Elements (page 19), pin and stitch the borders to the quilt.

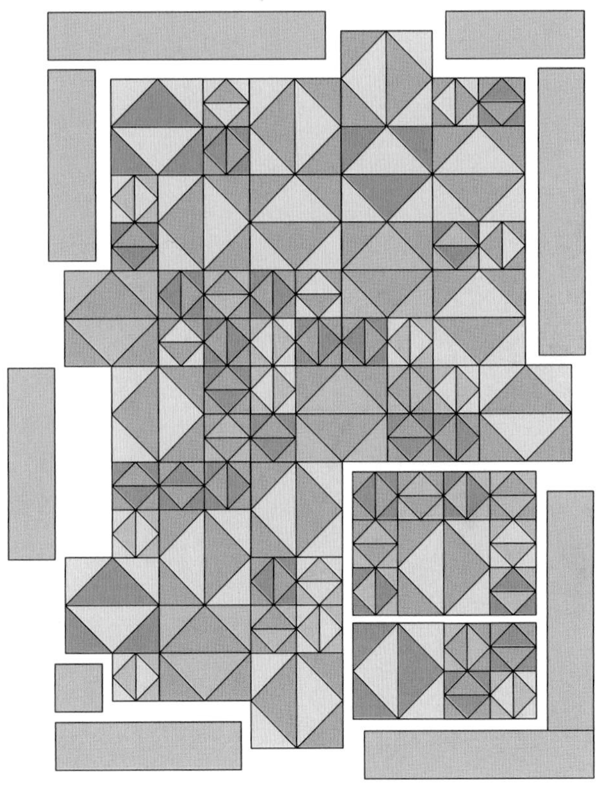

Assembly diagram

FINISHING

1. Refer to Quiltmaking Basics (page 74) to layer and baste your quilt and prepare it for quilting.
2. Quilt as desired. This quilt has been quilted in an allover swirling design.
3. From the remainder of the border and binding fabric, cut 5 strips 2¼″ × width of fabric.
4. Refer to Quiltmaking Basics to bind and finish your quilt.

Atlantis

Finished block sizes: 6″ × 6″, 12″ × 12″
Finished quilt size: 54″ × 78″

Vibrant hand-dyed fabrics in ocean colors combine with quilted "seaweed" designs to create a quilt reminiscent of the swirling sea and what lies beneath. With this interesting block combination, the smaller block is used as the center of the larger block. The simple angle created in the blocks also forms a diagonal pattern throughout the quilt, giving it visual movement.

Designed and pieced by Lisa Walton, and machine quilted by Nic Bridges, 2006

Fabric Requirements

Yardages are based on 44″-wide fabric.

2 yards of bright blue for borders, binding, and blocks

¾ yard of blue-green for blocks

¾ yard of light green for blocks

¾ yard of medium green for blocks

¾ yard of dark green for blocks

¾ yard of turquoise blue for blocks

½ yard of dark blue for blocks

3½ yards or a 60″ × 84″ piece for the backing

60″ × 84″ piece of batting

Cutting

WOF = width of fabric

From the bright blue fabric:

Cut 4 strips 2″ × WOF for the blocks.

Cut 2 strips 3½″ × WOF for the blocks.

Cut 7 strips 3½″ × WOF for the border.

Cut 7 strips 2¼″ × WOF for the binding.

From the dark blue fabric:

Cut 4 strips 2″ × WOF for the blocks.

Cut 2 strips 3½″ × WOF for the blocks.

From each of the other 5 block fabrics:

Cut 3 strips 3½″ × WOF.

Cut 7 strips 2″ × WOF.

Note

This quilt is made from hand-dyed fabrics, but you can easily substitute batiks or solids. This is essentially a scrap quilt, so any combination of analogous fabrics can be used for each block.

BLOCKS

You will need 10 large blocks and 66 small blocks.

Small blocks

These blocks are made with random combinations of all 7 block fabrics, so any of the 2″ strips can be used with a 3½″ × 3½″ square in the center.

1. From the strips, cut for each small block:

   1 square 3½″ × 3½″

   2 rectangles 2″ × 5″

   2 rectangles 2″ × 3½″

   4 squares 2″ × 2″

2. Stitch a 2″ × 3½″ rectangle to each side of a 3½″ square; press seams toward the rectangles.

3. Place a 2″ square on the 2″ × 5″ rectangle as shown and stitch across the diagonal. Trim the excess; turn and press.

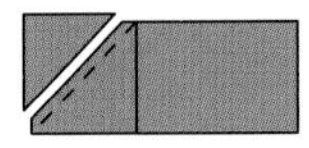

4. Stitch the other 2″ square to the other end of the rectangle.

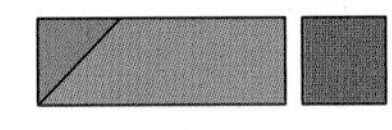

5. Repeat with the other 2″ × 5″ rectangle and the 2 remaining 2″ squares.

6. Join the units from Step 5 to the top and bottom of the block, and press seams toward the outside. Trim the block to 6½″ square.

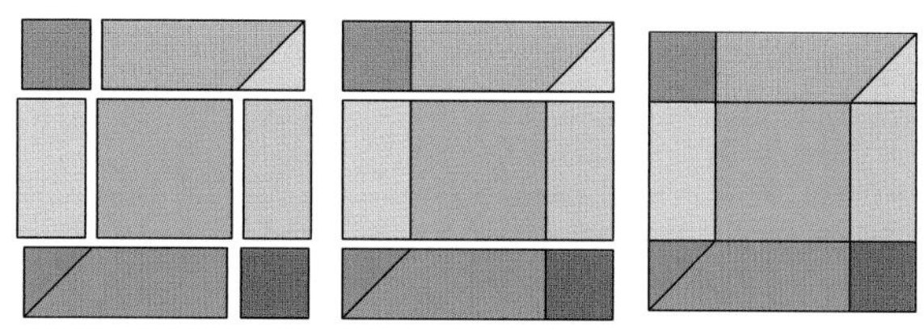

Small block construction

7. Repeat Steps 1–6 to make a total of 66 small blocks in different color combinations.

Large blocks

As with the small blocks, the large blocks are made with random combinations of fabrics. An already made small block forms the center of each large block.

1. From the 3½″ strips, cut the following for each large block:

 2 rectangles 3½″ × 9½″

 2 rectangles 3½″ × 6½″

 4 squares 3½ ″ × 3½″

2. Use a previously made small block and orient it so the diagonal formed by the triangles goes from the bottom left to the top right. Stitch a 3½″ × 6½″ rectangle to each side. Press seams toward the rectangles.

3. Place a 3½″ square on top of a 3½″ × 9½″ rectangle, and sew on the diagonal as shown in Small Blocks, Step 3. Trim the excess, turn, and press.

4. Stitch the other 3½″ square to the other end of the rectangle.

5. Repeat with the other 3½″ × 9½″ rectangle and the 2 remaining 3½″ squares.

6. Join the units from Step 5 to the top and bottom of the unit from Step 2, and press seams toward the outside. Trim the block to 12½″ square.

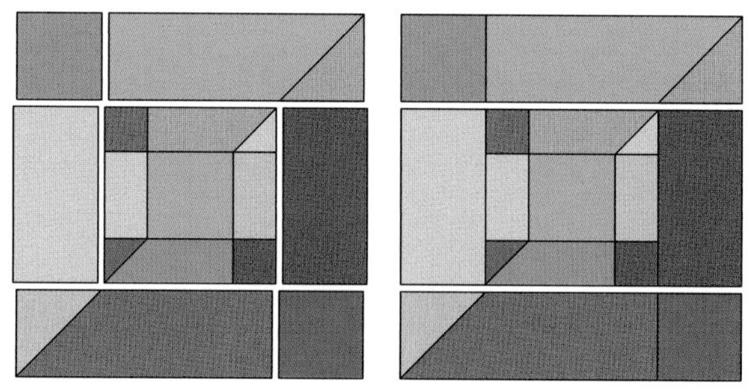

Large block construction

7. Repeat Steps 1–6 to make a total of 10 blocks in different color combinations.

QUILT TOP

Refer to the assembly diagram to lay out the blocks. This quilt uses a single-module structure: 4 small blocks form a 12½" square. This quilt is assembled in rows; the top and bottom rows are formed entirely by small blocks.

1. Stitch 8 small blocks together for the top row; repeat for the bottom row.
2. Stitch 4 small blocks together to form a 12½" square, making sure the diagonals are facing the same direction. Repeat to make a total of 10 modules 12½" square.
3. Stitch the 4-block module to a large block. Repeat for each large block, making sure to keep diagonals facing the same way.
4. Lay out 5 rows and the top and bottom rows as shown. Stitch the blocks together, and then stitch rows together.

Borders

This quilt has an interesting border treatment using half-square triangles to extend the strong diagonal design in the blocks.

1. From the 3½" border fabric strips, cut the following: a strip 6½", 2 strips 15½", 2 strips 18½", 5 strips 24½", and 2 strips 30½".
2. From the remaining block fabrics, cut 9 squares 3½" × 3½".
3. For the left side border, place a 3½" square on top of each 2 of the 24½" strips and the 6½" strip. Stitch along the diagonal as you did for the blocks, and trim the excess. Press.
4. Referring to the assembly diagram, join strips 18½", 24½", 24½", and 6½". This strip is the left side border.
5. Pin the border to the left side of the quilt, carefully matching seams. Stitch together, and press seams toward the border.
6. Make the right side border: Stitch a square diagonally to an 18½" and a 24½" strip, making sure the triangles will face the right way; then join this to a 30½" strip. Pin to the right side of the quilt, carefully matching seams. Stitch together, and press seams toward border.
7. Make the top border the same way: Stitch a square diagonally to a 24½" and a 30½" strip, making sure the triangles formed will face the right way. Pin border to top, stitch, and press toward border.
8. Finally, add the bottom border: Stitch a square diagonally to a 15½" strip and a 24½" strip, and join these to a 15½" strip. Pin, stitch, and press.

Assembly diagram

FINISHING

1. Refer to Quiltmaking Basics (page 74) to layer and baste your quilt to prepare it for quilting.
2. Quilt as desired. This quilt features an allover design called Big Splash, which is reminiscent of swirling seaweed. Other options for quilting would be to follow the straight diagonal lines created by the triangles.
3. Use the 2¼" binding strips and refer to Quiltmaking Basics to bind and finish your quilt.

Tip

If you would like to make this quilt in a different size, refer to Increasing Quilt Size (page 18).

Cornerstones

Finished block sizes: 8″ × 8″, 4″ × 4″
Finished quilt size: 80″ × 88″

This quilt uses two sizes of a very simple block, each with a corner square of white. Rotating the blocks in a random pattern lends this quilt a sense of movement. I chose to make it using solid fabrics in a range of warm, sunny colors varying from light to dark values.

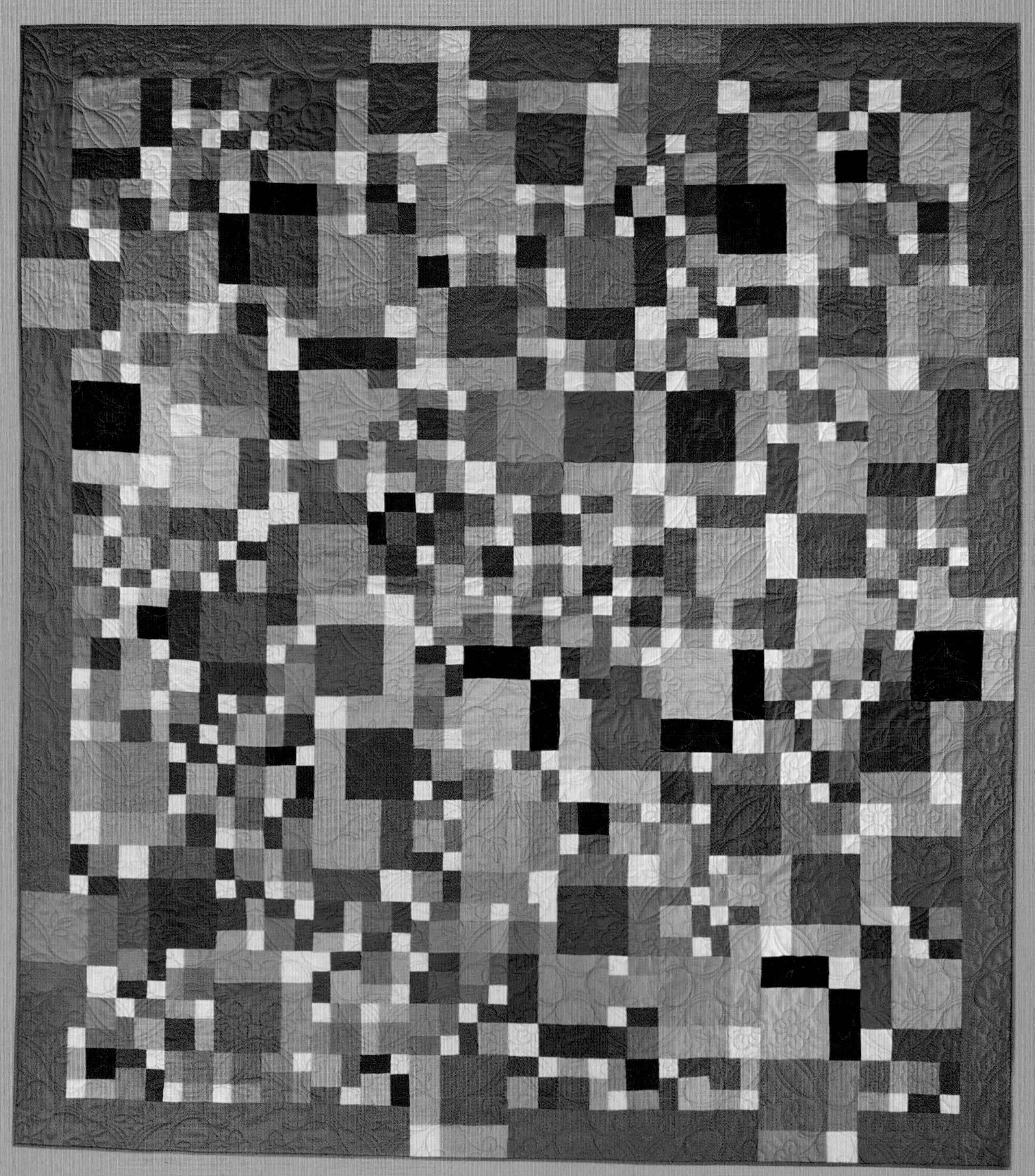

Designed and pieced by Lisa Walton, and machine quilted by Kimpossible Quilting, 2012

Fabric Requirements

Yardages are based on 44″-wide fabric.

22 fat quarters in analogous solids for the blocks*

1 yard of a light solid for the block corners*

1½ yards of a solid for the border and binding*

5⅜ yards or an 86″ × 94″ piece for the backing

86″ × 94″ batting

** I used a fat quarter bundle of Kona Cotton Solids in the Candy Corn colorstory. For the light corners, I chose Kona Cotton White. For the border and binding, I used School Bus, one of the colors in the bundle.*

Note

This quilt is designed using fat quarters (18″ × 22″), but cut yardage or scraps can be used equally effectively. Slightly patterned fabrics such as batiks would work well as an alternative to solids. For the block corners, choose a light color to create a feeling of lightness and clarity; a dark color will become too much of a dominating focus of the quilt.

Cutting

WOF = width of fabric

From the light solid for the corners:

Cut 8 strips 2″ × WOF; crosscut into 164 squares 2″ × 2″.

Cut 4 strips 3″ × WOF; crosscut into 53 squares.

From the border and binding fabric:

Cut 7 strips 4½″ × WOF for the border.

Cut 9 strips 2¼″ × WOF for the binding.

BLOCKS

You will need a total of 53 large blocks and 164 small blocks.

Cutting blocks

Follow the cutting diagrams to cut out block pieces from layered fat quarters.

1. For the large blocks, place 2 fat quarters together and cut as shown in cutting diagram A. Each pair of fat quarters yields 10 large blocks. Repeat 4 times for a total of 50 blocks.

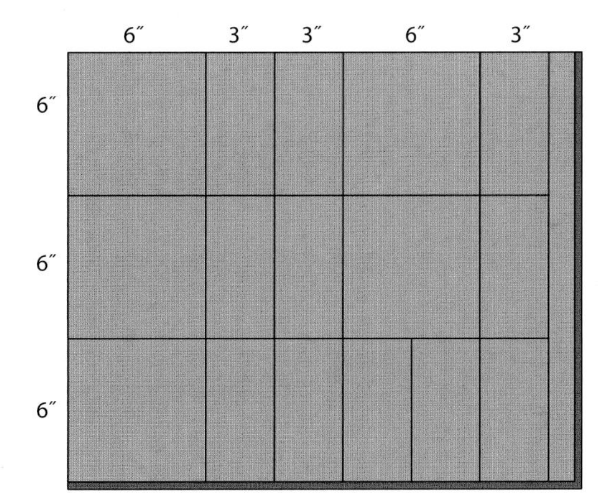

Cutting diagram A

2. For the small blocks, place 2 fat quarters together and follow cutting diagram B. Each pair of fat quarters yields 36 small blocks. Repeat 3 times for a total of 144 blocks.

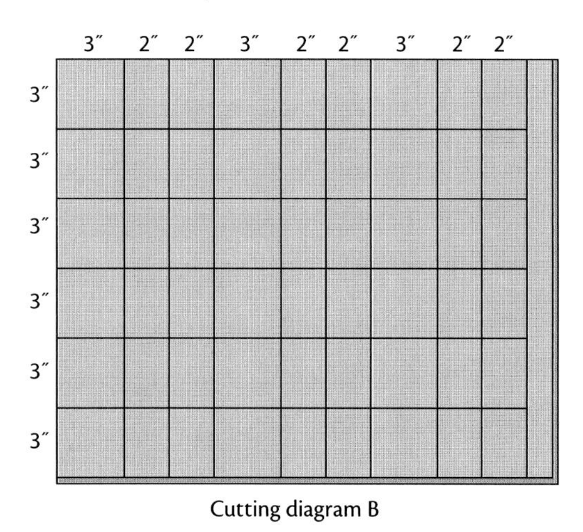

Cutting diagram B

3. To make the remaining blocks, place 2 fat quarters together and follow cutting diagram C. This yields 4 large blocks and 20 small blocks.

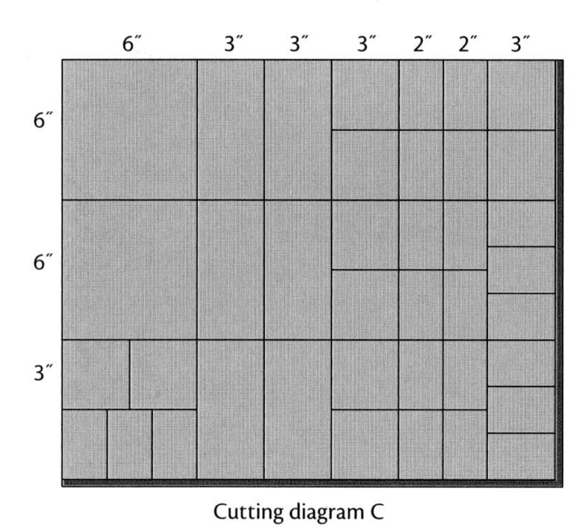

Cutting diagram C

4. If you find you need additional block pieces, use the 2 remaining fat quarters.

Making blocks

SMALL BLOCK

Each small block requires a light square 2″ × 2″, 2 rectangles 2″ × 3″ of the same fabric, and a square 3″ × 3″ of a different fabric.

1. Stitch a 2″ light square to a 2″ × 3″ rectangle.

2. Stitch the 3″ square to the other 2″ × 3″ rectangle.

3. Pin to match seams, and stitch together to form the small block.

4. Press the seams away from the light fabric, and trim block to 4½″ × 4½″.

LARGE BLOCK

Each large block requires a light square 3″ × 3″, 2 rectangles 3″ × 6″ of the same fabric, and a square 6″ × 6″ of a different fabric.

1. Stitch a 3″ light square to a 3″ × 6″ rectangle.

2. Stitch a 6″ square to the other 3″ × 6″ rectangle.

3. Pin to match seams, and stitch together to form the large block.

4. Press the seams away from the light fabric, and trim block to 8½″ × 8½″.

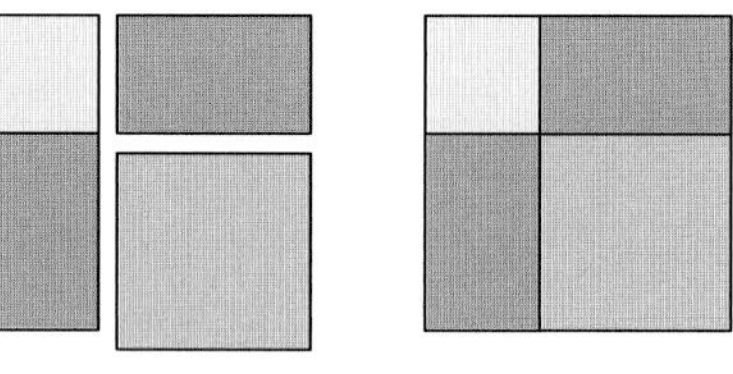

Block construction

Note

When you have made a few blocks, you can start to experiment by laying four to six fat quarters together and mixing and matching color combinations.

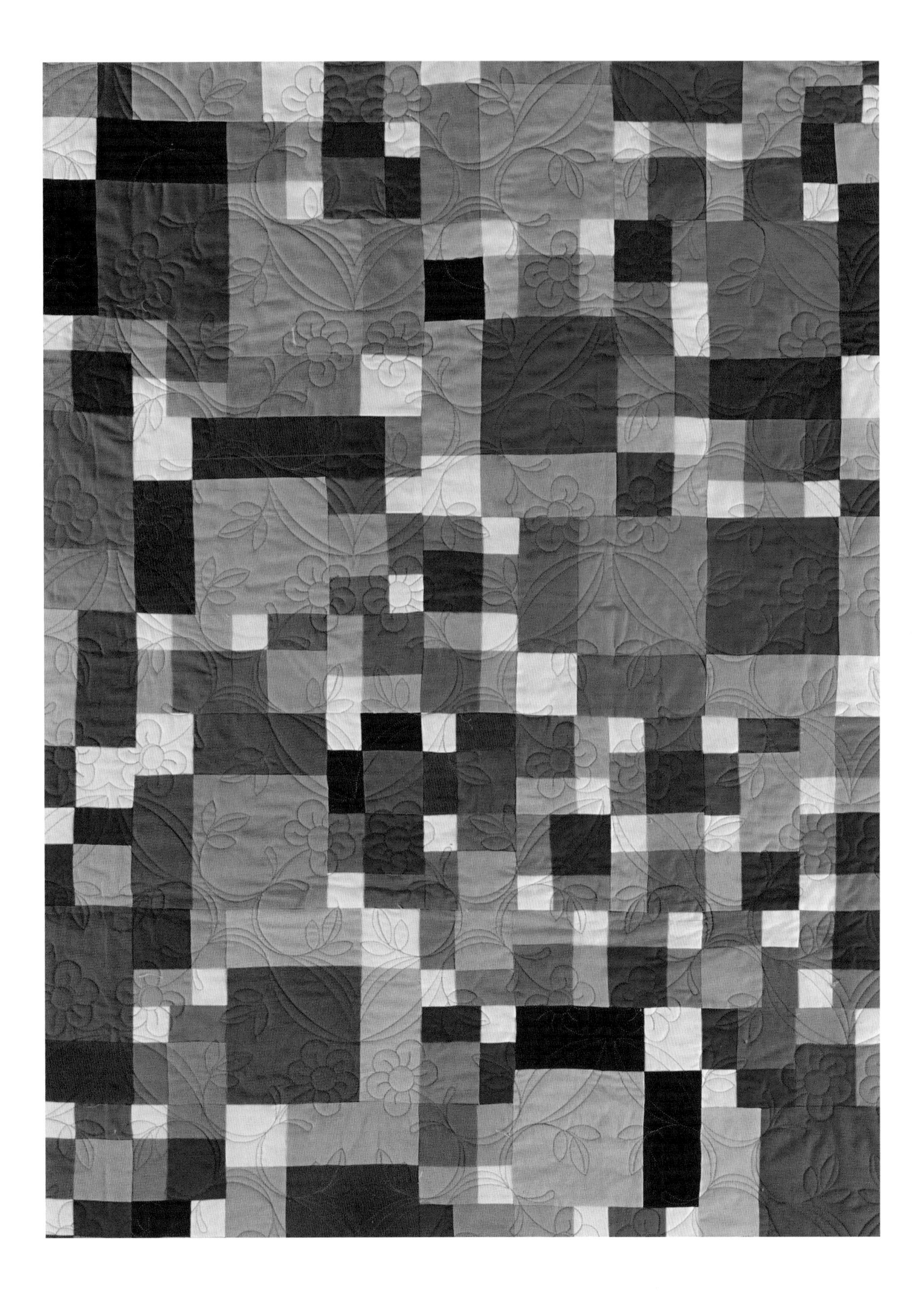

QUILT TOP

As shown in Breaking Down the Designs (page 8) it is very easy to change the feel of the quilt by either lining up all the blocks to give a very geometric feel or rotating the blocks randomly to create a more free-form design.

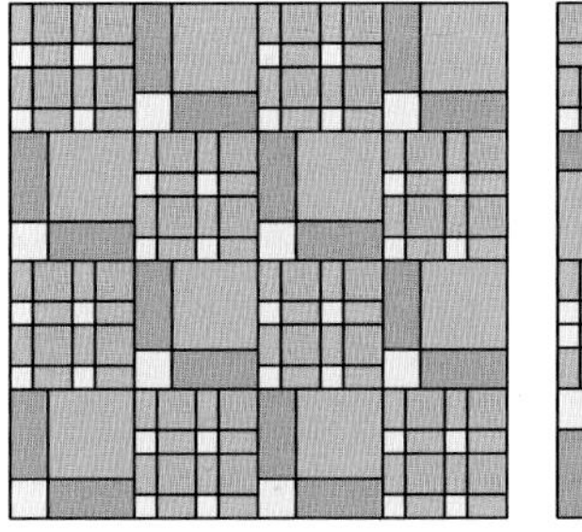

At left, all blocks are oriented the same way; at right, some blocks are rotated.

At left, blocks are placed randomly but facing the same way; at right, blocks are placed randomly and rotated randomly.

To make this quilt as shown, refer to the assembly diagram. For this quilt layout you will need 53 large blocks and 164 small blocks.

Borders

This border treatment features 8 blocks extending into the borders.

1. If you created your own layout, measure and cut border strips according to your design. If following the layout in *Cornerstones*, cut each of the following lengths from the 4½″ border strips: 8½″, 28½″, 44½″, 24½″, and 36½″. Cut 2 each of 12½″ and 16½″ lengths. Cut 3 strips 20½″.

2. Following the instructions in Borders as Design Elements (page 19), pin and stitch the borders to the quilt.

FINISHING

1. Refer to Quiltmaking Basics (page 74) to layer and baste your quilt to prepare it for quilting.

2. Quilt as desired. This quilt has a lovely, swirly allover floral design done on a longarm machine. Another option would be to do straight stitching on a domestic machine, traveling between the intersections in the blocks and changing direction each time you meet a new block.

3. Refer to Quiltmaking Basics to bind and finish your quilt.

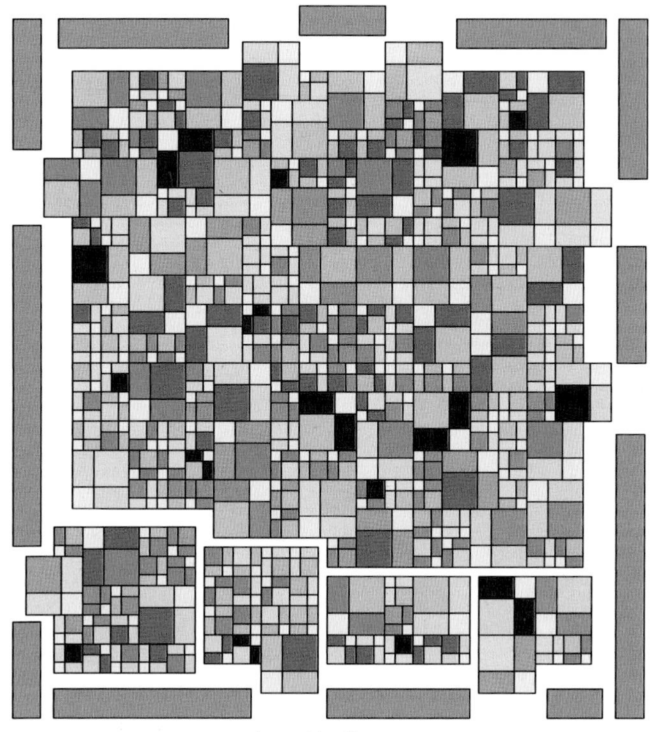

Assembly diagram

Any Which Way

Finished block size: 16″ × 16″

Finished quilt size: 88″ × 88″

Leap, and the net will appear. I am not one for cute phrases, but this one has always appealed to me. Why not use this quilt as your leap into the unknown? The time has come for you to really start playing. I am going to give you guidelines for this quilt—but really you can put together the units and blocks any way you want.

This quilt uses squares and rectangles that interlink to create a dynamic design. It is made up of two main colors, plus an exciting contrasting fabric used in the border and in a smaller quantity within the body of the quilt to create continuity and highlights. The fabrics are batik "stripes" that aren't quite straight; this really adds to the quirky nature of the quilt.

Designed and pieced by Lisa Walton, and machine quilted by Kimpossible Quilting, 2012

Fabric Requirements

Yardages are based on 44″-wide fabric.

3¾ yards of purple striped batik for the blocks and binding*

2½ yards of raspberry striped batik for the blocks

2 yards of orange striped batik for the zinger blocks and borders*

8 yards or a 94″ × 94″ piece for the backing

94″ × 94″ piece of batting

** I used Elementals by Lunn Studios for Robert Kaufman Artisan Batiks in Purple, Raspberry, and Red.*

Note

When I started this quilt, I selected three fabrics that I liked and just started cutting. I had no idea what it would look like when finished. I love this process and would encourage you to give it a try.

From experience, I know that a quilt around 80″ × 80″ uses about nine yards of fabric. I always make sure to have a little more if I am working in this serendipitous way. This is a simple pieced quilt with fairly large pieces, but if you made a more complex quilt with tiny pieces, you would need more fabric, because quite a lot of fabric is used in the seam allowances.

You can always wait until the quilt is finished to calculate the backing fabric and batting required.

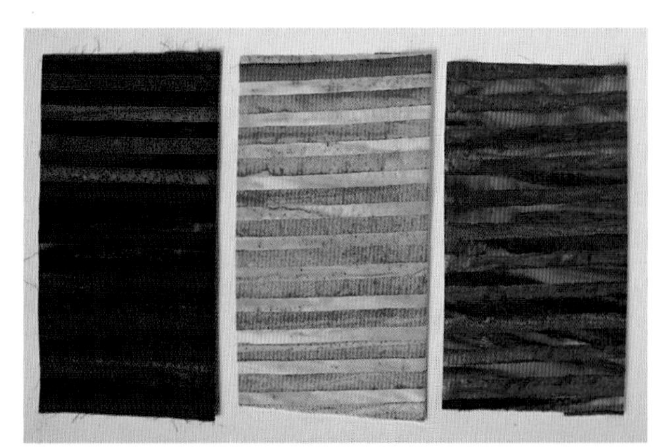

Stripes work well in designs with simple shapes.

PLANNING THE QUILT

This quilt has 25 blocks set into 5 rows of 5 blocks each. Each block is laid out differently and is made up of squares in 2 sizes, as well as rectangles. This allows for a seemingly endless number of configurations.

For this quilt, I decided to use raspberry and purple as the main colors and use orange for zing. I realized that the orange strips would need to be smaller because of their dominating color, yet I still needed them to fit into the grid concept. The purple and raspberry squares and rectangles are based on 4″ and 8″, so I decided all the orange strips would be 2″ × 8″. This meant two orange strips would equal a 4″ × 8″ rectangle. Thus, I knew I would need an even number of these orange strips.

I decided to use orange in the border as well. I made the border 4″ wide to allow the 4″ × 8″ rectangles to extend into the border as described in Borders as Design Elements (page 19).

Cutting

I didn't cut all the fabric at once. I just cut a selection from each of the two main fabrics and started playing. As shown in the suggested cutting diagram, I cut the block rectangles in two directions. This allowed some to have stripes going horizontally and some vertically. Following are the amounts I wound up using for this quilt.

WOF = width of fabric

From the purple striped batik:

Cut 18 squares 8½″ × 8½″ for the blocks.

Cut 41 squares 4½″ × 4½″ for the blocks.

Cut 44 rectangles 4½″ × 8½″ for the blocks.

Cut 9 strips 2¼″ × WOF for the binding.

From the raspberry striped batik:

Cut 16 squares 8½″ × 8½″ for the blocks.

Cut 33 squares 4½″ × 4½″ for the blocks.

Cut 29 rectangles 4½″ × 8½″ for the blocks.

From the orange striped batik:

(See Note below.)

Cut 10 strips 4½″ × WOF for the border strips.

Cut 7 strips 8½″ × width of remaining fabric; crosscut into 56 rectangles 2½″ × 8½″ for the blocks.

Note

The border strips should run the same way as the stripes, so depending on the fabric, you may need to cut them lengthwise, but the fabric requirement is the same. My batik stripe ran across the width of fabric. I cut the border strips first so that I wouldn't accidentally use them in the quilt!

BLOCKS

As I made it, this quilt has 25 blocks. Each block has many possible combinations using the simple squares and rectangles. I usually work with a predetermined module size to make it easier to join blocks. In this case, I first made 8″ × 16″ modules and joined them together to form a 16″ × 16″ block.

Remember that if you want to extend blocks into the border, make at least 4 of these (I used 8), so there is a block on each side of the quilt for balance. Also set aside 2 squares 4½″ × 4½″ of both of the 2 main colors for the corner blocks.

Some block layout combinations

1. Arrange and sew together the purple, raspberry, and orange squares and rectangles in a random pattern to create 50 units 8½″ × 16½″, including 8 blocks with a rectangle extending out.

2. Join the 8½″ × 16½″ units together to form 25 blocks 16½″ × 16½″.

QUILT TOP

Refer to the assembly diagram, or lay out the blocks in your own design.

1. Stitch 5 blocks together in a row, with the blocks extending to the outside for the top.

2. Repeat for the bottom row, ensuring that the extending blocks are not directly opposite the ones at the top.

3. Join the remaining 15 blocks into 3 rows of 5, ensuring that the extending blocks are not in the same row on both sidess.

4. Pin carefully to match seams where possible, and stitch the rows together.

Borders

This border treatment features 8 blocks extending into the borders, with a square at each corner.

Tip

When you are making a large quilt with long borders, you may not want to have to join border pieces. To avoid this, make sure that there are no border sections longer than about 40″ between the extending blocks.

1. From the 4½″ border strips, cut the following lengths: 2 strips 32½″, 3 strips 28½″, 3 strips 24½″, 3 strips 20½″, and 1 strip 8½″.

2. Following the instructions in Borders as Design Elements (page 19), pin and stitch the borders to the quilt.

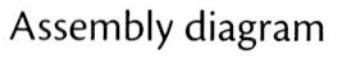

Assembly diagram

FINISHING

1. Refer to Quiltmaking Basics (page 74) to layer and baste your quilt to prepare it for quilting.

2. Quilt as desired. This quilt has been machine quilted in an allover feather design.

3. Using the 9 strips 2¼″ of binding fabric, bind your quilt, referring to Quiltmaking Basics.

Bonus Project:

Round the Corner Wallhanging

Finished block sizes: 8″ × 8″, 4″ × 4″, 1″ × 4″

Finished quilt size: 44″ × 44″

This wallhanging is a smaller version of *Any Which Way*. The fabric is a single piece of cotton sateen that I painted with dye in a gradation from green to lemon yellow, then orange, then red. After the fabric was finished, I decided not to use the reddest portion because the color was too strong. The intense orange became the zinger fabric. The very red portion? It will be used another day.

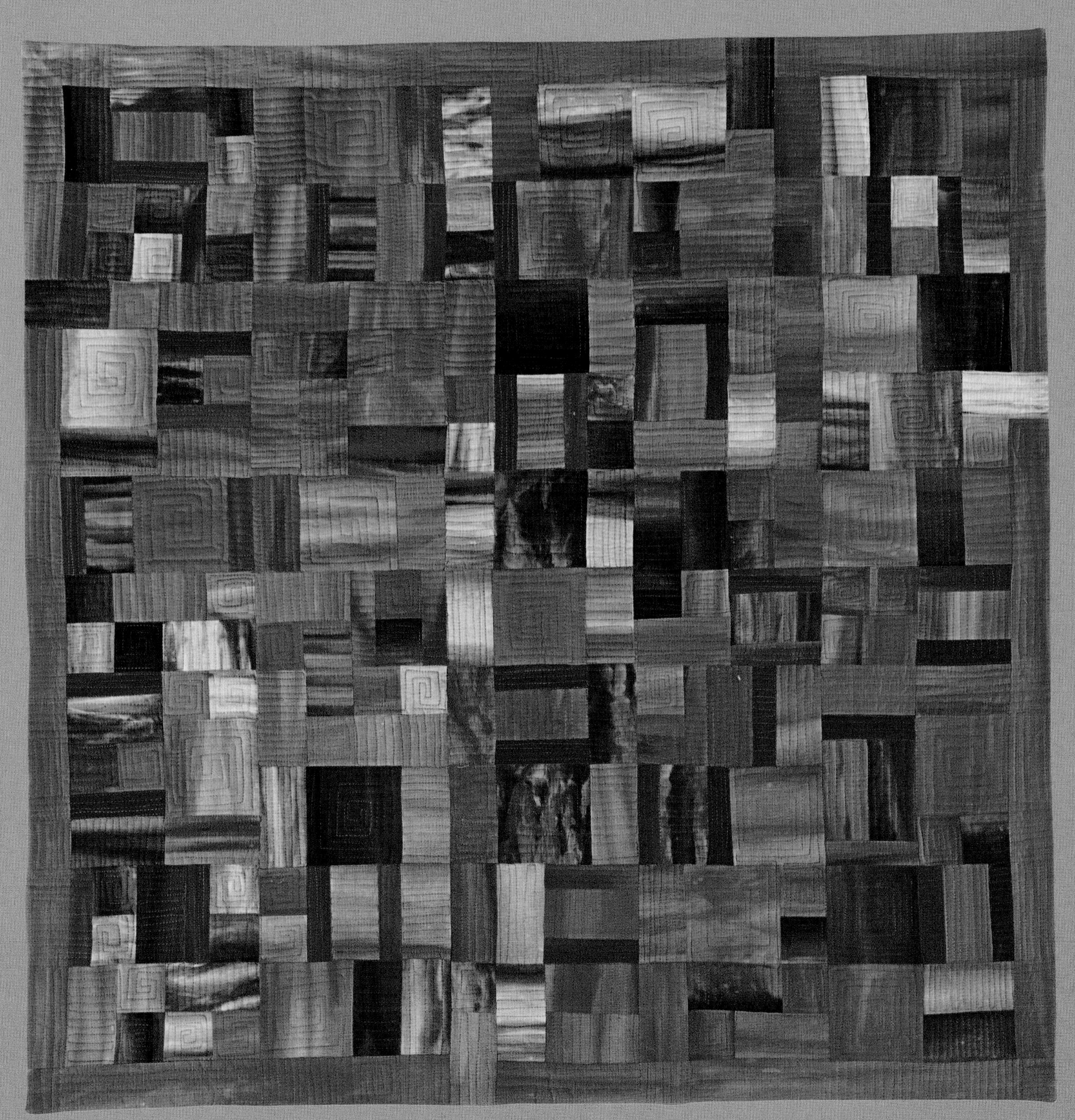

Designed, pieced, and quilted by Lisa Walton, 2012

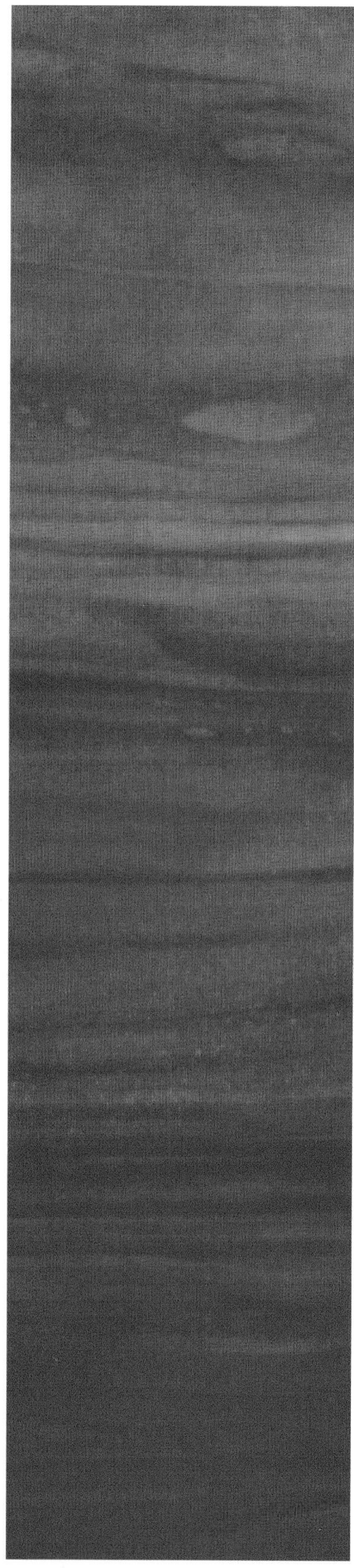

Fabric hand painted with dye by the author

Fabric Requirements

Yardages are based on 44″-wide fabric.

2½ yards of hand dyes, batiks, or mottled solids gradated from lemon yellow to deep green for the blocks, borders, and facing

⅜ yard of orange zinger fabric for the blocks (See Split complementary, page 12)

2⅞ yards or a 50″ × 50″ piece of fabric for the backing

50″ × 50″ piece of batting

Note

If hand-dyed fabrics are unavailable, you may choose from many other fabrics that are made to look like hand dyes. Batiks are also suitable. You may need to buy a few different fabrics to create the same contrasting effect.

My hand-painted fabric was 108″ wide; I used approximately 1½ yards of it to make this quilt and used the remainder for the backing. This is equivalent to approximately 4 yards of 40″-wide commercial fabric.

PLANNING THE QUILT

Because this quilt was made from a single piece of fabric in gradated colors, I planned how to cut it so that I would get certain pieces from certain areas of the fabric. I wanted blocks made up of units from the yellow and green areas, with small strips of the orange for zingers, and yellow for the border.

In this smaller version of *Any Which Way*, it was necessary to reduce the scale of the blocks. If I had kept the same size blocks, the quilt would not look so interesting. So the finished sizes cut from the main fabric are 4″ × 4″, 2″ × 2″, and 2″ × 4″.

Because I halved the dimensions of each basic unit, I also needed to halve the orange to 1″ × 4″. Small slivers of the orange keep your eyes moving around the quilt and give it interest.

With wallhangings of this size, the width of the fabric is usually a good gauge for the final size and thus for how long the borders will be. So I cut four border strips, 2½″ wide, across the fabric width. This 2″-finished width is also the size of the rectangles that extend into the border.

The facing strips are 2¼″ wide and the same length as the border, so I cut four facing strips. I used a green section of the hand-dyed fabric, but you can cut facing strips from any of the available colors.

Cutting

As with *Any Which Way* (page 53), I cut blocks as I went, as needed. This gave me more flexibility with the design, especially if I changed my mind along the way.

WOF = width of fabric

From the yellow-to-green fabric:

Cut 14 strips 4½″ wide; crosscut into:

24 squares 4½″ × 4½″

92 rectangles 2½″ × 4½″

Cut 5 strips 2½″ × WOF; crosscut into 82 squares 2½″ × 2½″.

Cut 4 strips 2½″ × WOF for the borders.

Cut 4 strips 2¼″ × WOF for the facing.

From the orange fabric:

Cut 6 strips 1½″ × WOF; crosscut into 42 rectangles 1½″ × 4½″.

BLOCKS

Like *Any Which Way*, this quilt has 25 blocks. The blocks contain squares in two different sizes, as well as rectangles, which can be put together in a number of configurations.

To make the blocks, follow the instructions for *Any Which Way*.

For this version, you will need to arrange the squares and rectangles into 50 modules 4½″ × 8½″. Put these together to create 25 blocks 8½″ × 8½″. If you wish to have blocks extending into the border, make 4 blocks with a rectangle extending. See Borders as Design Elements (page 19).

QUILT TOP

To make the quilt top as shown, refer to the assembly diagram and, if needed, the Quilt Top assembly steps for *Any Which Way* (page 56).

Borders

1. Cut the 2½″ border strips into the following lengths: 8½″, 18½″, 24½″, and 26½″. Cut 2 strips each of the following lengths: 12½″ and 30½″.

2. Following the instructions in Borders as Design Elements (page 19), pin and stitch the borders to the quilt.

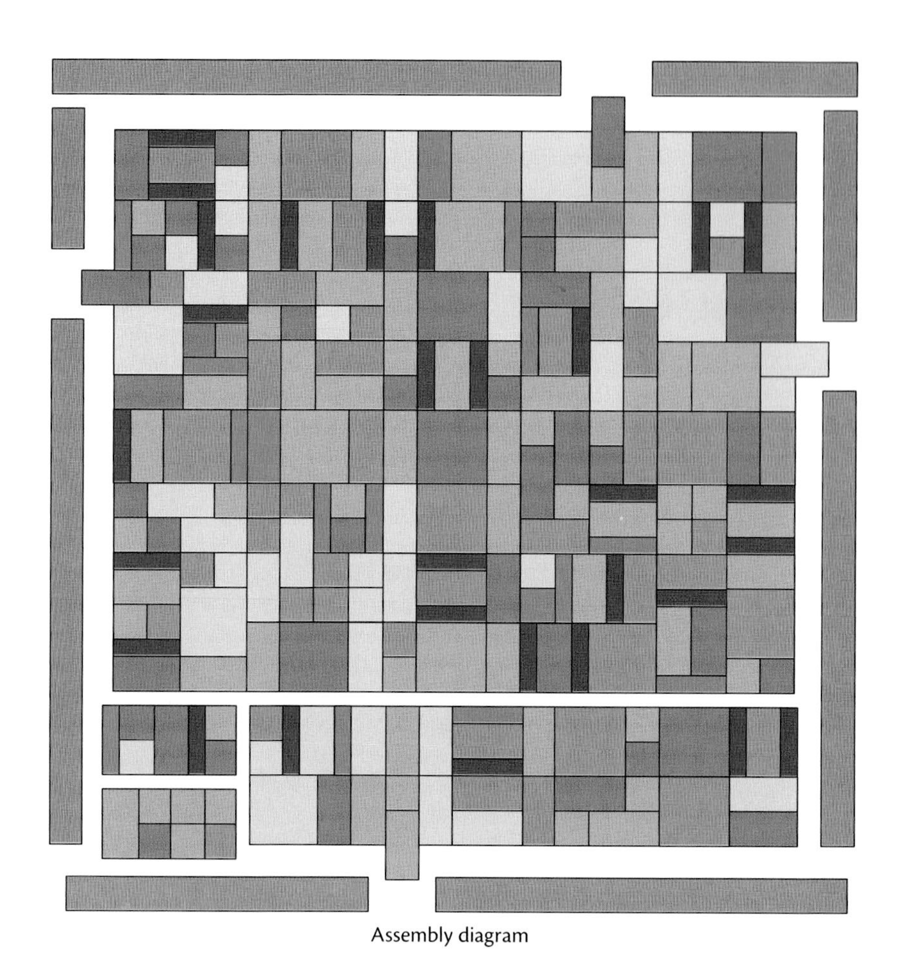

Assembly diagram

FINISHING

1. Refer to Quiltmaking Basics (page 74) to layer and baste your quilt to prepare it for quilting.

2. Quilt as desired. *Round the Corner Wallhanging* was quilted with blocks of parallel lines and square spirals.

3. Using the 4 facing strips 2¼″, finish your quilt, referring to Quiltmaking Basics.

Wobbling Windows

Finished block sizes: 6″ × 6″, 6″ × 3″, 3″ × 3″

Finished quilt size: 54″ × 51″

Sometimes you buy a fabric just because you love it: This batik was such a fabric. I loved the wonkiness of the striped design as well as the color gradations. I had only four yards, and I wanted to use only this fabric for the whole quilt. So how does one approach a challenge like this?

Designed and pieced by Lisa Walton, and machine quilted by Kimpossible Quilting, 2012

Fabric Requirements

Yardages are based on 44″-wide fabric.

Brown, purple, and teal strips were cut from this single batik fabric for this quilt.

1¾ yards of brown for blocks and borders*

1⅝ yards of purple for blocks and binding

1½ yards of teal for blocks

3¼ yards or a 60″ × 57″ piece for the backing

60″ × 57″ piece of batting

** I used Patina Handpaints by Lunn Studios for Robert Kaufman Artisan Batiks in Harvest, which has stripes in three colors: brown, purple, and teal. The above fabric requirements are given by color so that you can use three separate fabrics to make this quilt.*

Note

From experience I know that about four yards of fabric will make a wallhanging quilt of this size (approximately 50″ × 50″), depending on the number of seams and seam allowances. Smaller blocks create more seams, and therefore more fabric is lost in the seam allowances.

You can also always wait until the quilt is finished to calculate the backing fabric and batting required.

PLANNING THE QUILT

Think about the fabric—how much you have, and how you are going to cut it up. My striped batik fabric had three colors, so it seemed obvious that I should use them separately. If I had just made every block a combination of all three colors, the quilt would have had no focus.

I wanted to take advantage of the strong directional lines in the fabric by creating block centers with frames around them. I wanted the block centers to be on the diagonal to avoid having too many horizontal and vertical lines. Another important design decision was the frame width, because I wanted to use the same width for each block. I decided on a finished width of ¾″, because 1″ looked too wide for the smaller blocks.

I based the building blocks on 3″ and 6″, and drafted the three blocks on graph paper.

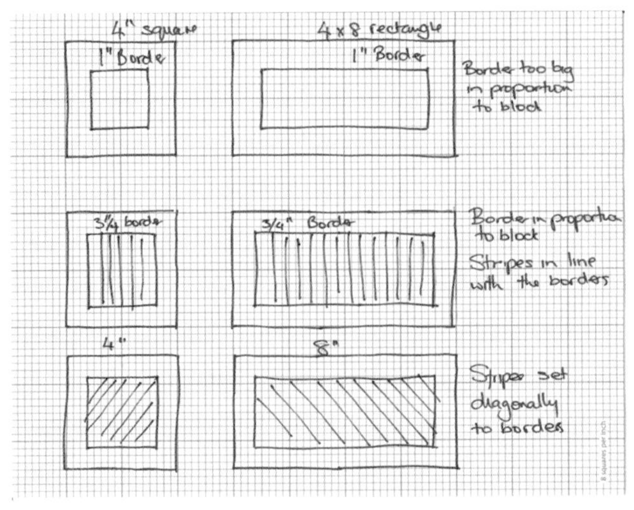

Drafting the blocks

Tip

Cutting fabric on the diagonal results in pieces that have a lot of stretch because they are cut on the bias. Extra care must be taken to avoid distortion when stitching. Don't use steam when pressing blocks with bias pieces.

The modules in this quilt are created by placing blocks of a certain color around blocks of a different color. This quilt has two module sizes: 12½″ × 12½″ and 9½″ × 12½″. I knew I wanted to have blocks extend into the border, so I took that into consideration and made four modules with extending rectangles.

Cutting

WOF = width of fabric

From the brown fabric:

Cut 17 strips 1¼″ × WOF for the block frames.

Cut 6 strips 3½″ × WOF for the borders.

From the purple fabric:

Cut 18 strips 1¼″ × WOF for the block frames.

Cut 6 strips 2¼″ × WOF for the binding.

From the teal fabric:

Cut 21 strips 1¼″ × WOF for the block frames.

Cutting the bias blocks

1. From the brown fabric, cut a strip 16″ × WOF.
2. Draw a diagonal line at 45° with a chalk marker, as shown. Follow the cutting diagram to cut squares and rectangles on the bias. For brown, you need 26 squares 2″ × 2″, 18 rectangles 2″ × 5″, and 4 squares 5″ × 5″.

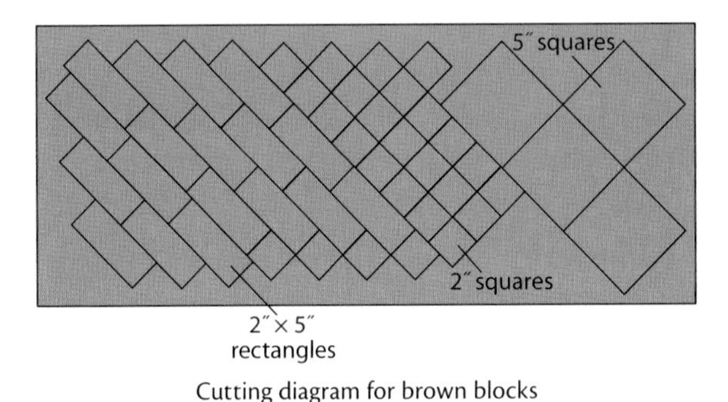

Cutting diagram for brown blocks

3. From the teal fabric, cut a strip 20″ × WOF. Mark the diagonal line as before, and cut 22 squares 2″ × 2″, 27 rectangles 2″ × 5″, and 4 squares 5″ × 5″.
4. From the purple fabric, cut a strip 18″ × WOF. Mark the diagonal line as before, and cut 20 squares 2″ × 2″, 25 rectangles 2″ × 5″, and a square 5″ × 5″.

Tip

The above cutting instructions for the bias blocks are provided so you can produce *Wobbling Windows* as shown, but every fabric is different and this is your original quilt. Don't cut all the fabric at once. Cut a selection from each of the three colors to start creating blocks.

BLOCKS

To create the layout in *Wobbling Windows*, you will need the following blocks:

Finished block size	Purple	Brown	Teal
3″ × 3″	20	26	22
3″ × 6″	25	18	27
6″ × 6″	1	4	4

1. To construct the blocks, first cut frame strips from the previously cut 1¼″ strips:
   - For the 3″ × 3″ block, cut 2 strips 1¼″ × 2″ and 2 strips 1¼″ × 3½″.
   - For the 3″ × 6″ block, cut 2 strips 1¼″ × 2″ and 2 strips 1¼″ × 6½″.
   - For the 6″ × 6″ block, cut 2 strips 1¼″ × 5″ and 2 strips 1¼″ × 6½″.
2. Stitch the shorter frame pieces to the top and bottom of the block, and press seams toward borders.
3. Stitch the longer frame pieces to the sides, and press seams toward borders.
4. Create blocks, stopping frequently to check your layout and decide on placement and color. Your block counts may vary from mine.

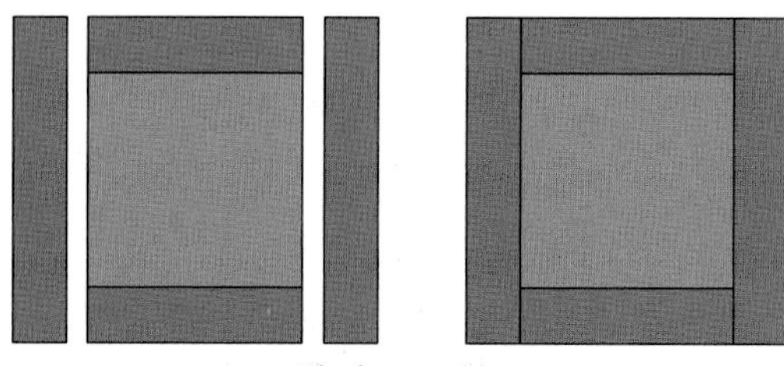

Block assembly

QUILT TOP

Refer to the assembly diagram, or lay out the blocks in your own design.

1. For the first row, stitch together 3 modules 12½″ × 12½″ and a module 9½″ × 12½″, extending a rectangle into the border.
2. Repeat 3 times for a total of 4 rows.
3. Pin carefully at the seams, and stitch the rows together.

Borders

The border corners are mitered, so you need to add 2″ to each border strip size. As a general rule you should add twice the width of the border and an extra 2″ to the border length.

1. From the 3½″ border strips cut the following lengths: 14½″, 17½″, 20½″, 23½″, 29½″, 32½″, 38½″, and 41½″.
2. Pin the border strips to the quilt top and stitch in place, starting and ending ¼″ from each end. Press the seam allowance toward the border.

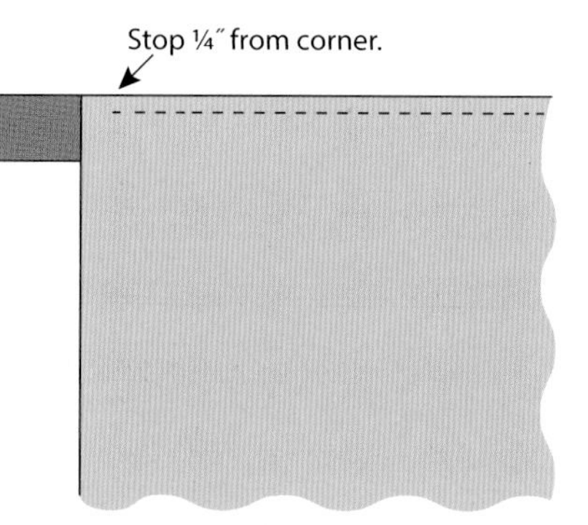

3. Overlap the border strips at a corner and mark the 45° angle on both sides.

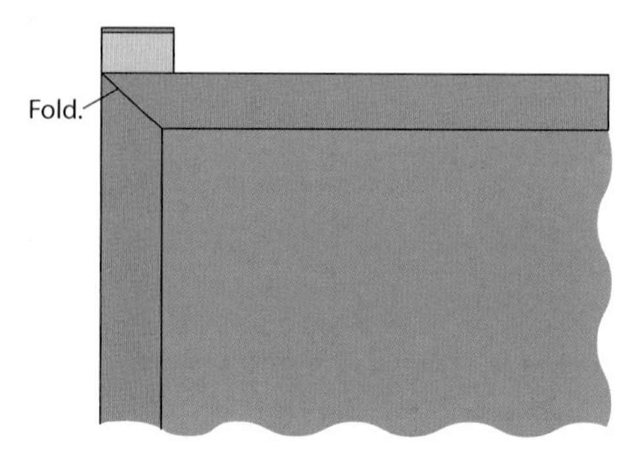

4. With right sides together, match these lines and pin in place.

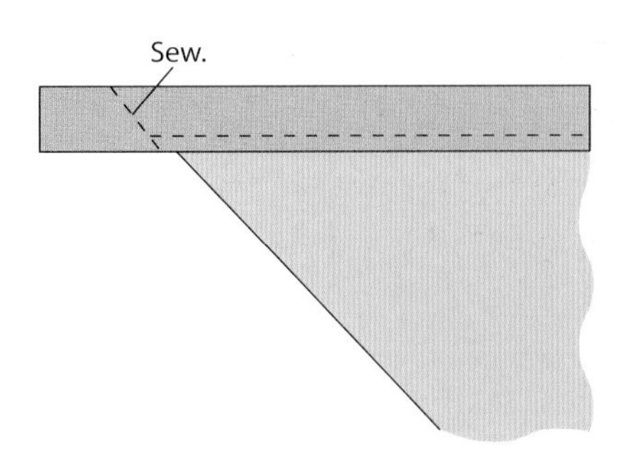

5. Stitch from the corner to the outside edge. Open out, check that it is square, and then trim the excess fabric.

6. Repeat with the other corners.

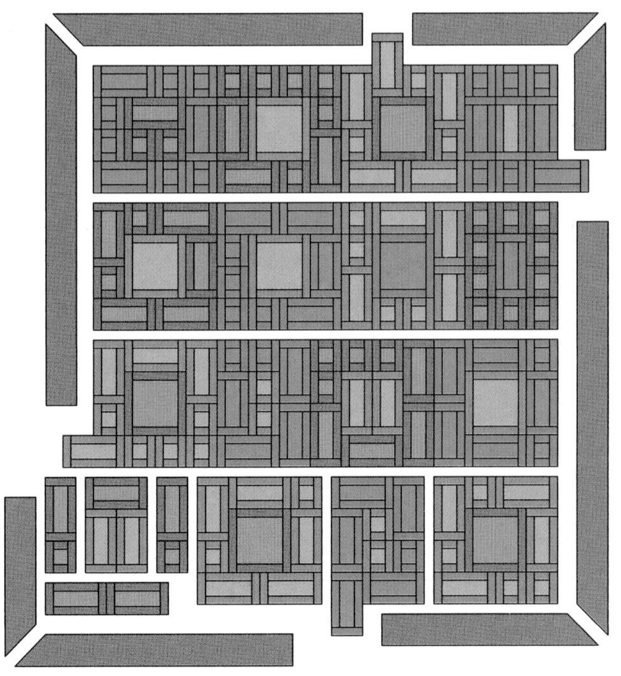

Assembly diagram

FINISHING

1. Refer to Quiltmaking Basics (page 74) to layer and baste your quilt to prepare it for quilting.

2. Quilt as desired. Here, an allover design was machine quilted. Other options are square spirals in each window or free-motion quilting across the diagonal lines of each block, changing direction in line with the blocks.

3. Using the 6 strips of 2¼″ binding fabric, bind your quilt, referring to Quiltmaking Basics.

Slashed

Finished basic block units: 1½″, 3″, and 6″ rectangles (3 sizes)
Finished quilt size: 48″ × 51″

The fabric in this quilt is a single piece of cotton sateen that I painted with dye in a gradation from deep fuchsia to lemon yellow.

The original fabric was 108″ wide, and I used approximately 1½ yards of it for this quilt. This is equivalent to approximately 4 yards of 40″-wide commercial fabric.

Designed and pieced by Lisa Walton, and machine quilted by Kimpossible Quilting, 2012

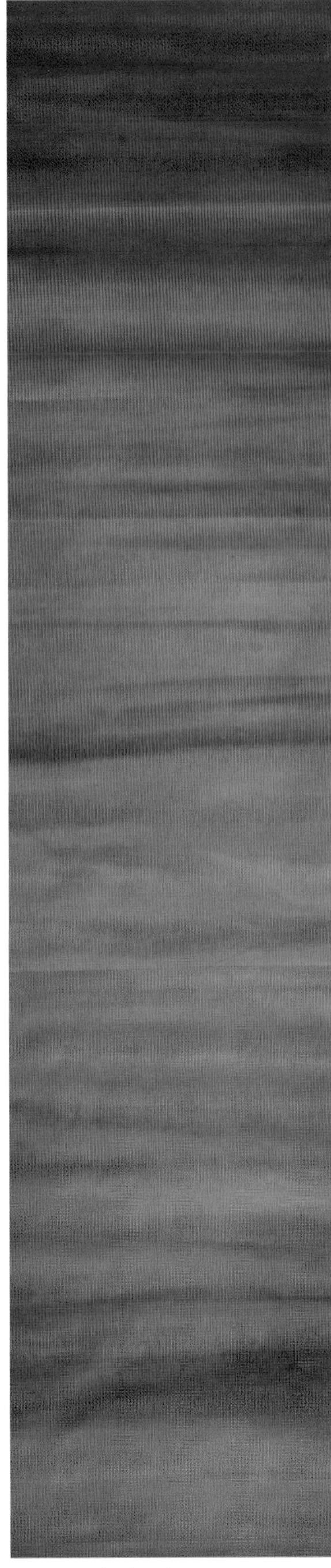

Hand-painted cotton sateen

Fabric Requirements

Yardages are based on 44″-wide fabric.

3¼ yards of batiks or hand dyes in pinks ranging from coral to fuchsia for the blocks and facing

¾ yard of yellow zinger fabric for the blocks

3 yards or a 54″ × 57″ piece for the backing

54″ × 57″ piece of batting

PLANNING THE QUILT

You will need to think about the fabric—how much of it you have and how you are going to cut it up. My hand-painted fabric had a smooth gradation of colors, and I wanted to use that flow in the quilt. I inserted slashes of a bright zinger color to help with the visual flow. The yellow fabric was a very strong color that I felt would act as a focal point.

Note

If you are unable to purchase hand-dyed fabrics, you can choose from many commercial fabrics that look like hand dyes. You can also choose from a wide range of batiks. You could also make this quilt in a gradated range of solids. You may need to buy a few different fabrics to create the same subtle effect.

From experience I know that four yards of fabric will make a wallhanging-size quilt around 40″ × 40″ to 50″ × 50″, depending on the number of seams and seam allowances. Smaller blocks create more seams, and therefore more fabric is lost in the seam allowances.

You can also always wait until the quilt is finished to calculate the backing fabric and batting required.

Cutting

WOF = width of fabric

From gradated pink fabrics:

Cut 6 strips 10″ × WOF; crosscut each into 2 rectangles 10″ × 20″ (or 22″ depending on fabric width).

Cut 4 strips 3½″ × WOF for the borders.*

Cut 5 strips 3″ × WOF for the facing.

From the yellow fabric:

Cut a strip 24″ × WOF; from this, crosscut strips 1½″ × 24″.

** If you want the borders to flow, depending on how the fabric is gradated, you may want to wait and cut borders later.*

BLOCKS

1. Cut the 10″ × 20″ strip into 3 parts, using wonky angles as shown.

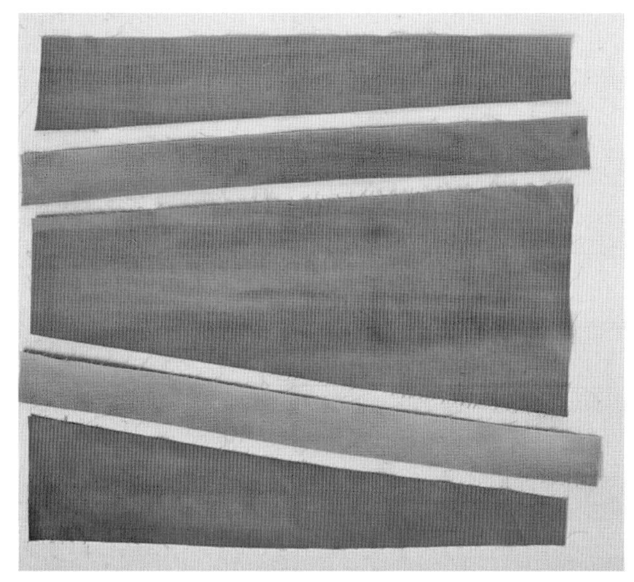

Cut strip into 3 parts.

2. Stitch the 1½″ yellow zinger strips between the sections as shown. Carefully press the seams toward the pink.
3. Crosscut this unit into 6½″, 3½″, and 2″ strips.

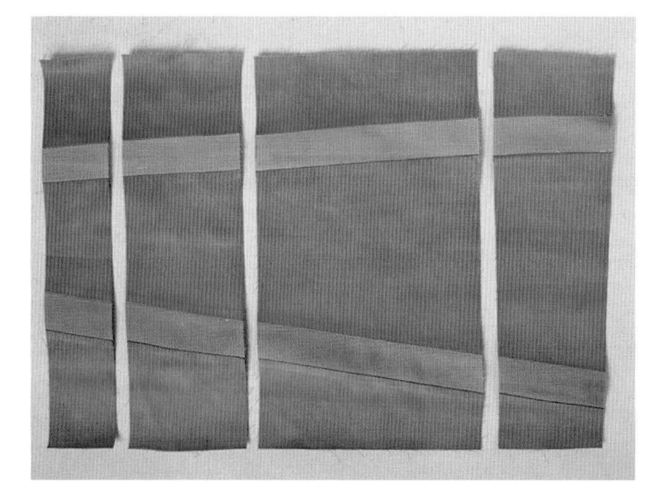

Crosscut pieced unit.

4. Trim lengths of the blocks to 9½″.
5. Repeat Steps 1–4 using the remaining 11 pink 10″ × 20″ strips. Your strip widths will vary from mine, but just for reference, *Slashed* contains about 12 strips 6″, 35 strips 3″, and 28 strips 1″.

QUILT TOP

Refer to the assembly diagram (page 69), or lay out the blocks in your own design.

1. Lay out the blocks on a design wall or a flat surface, and play with the combinations. It is unlikely that you will have the exact number of correctly sized blocks, so here is your opportunity to be creative.

Note

If you look very closely at my quilt, you might see that I made many diversions from the original three-block designs. Some blocks were cut down to 3½″ × 3½″ squares and 3½″ × 6½″ rectangles to fit a space. This is okay! You can do it, too! I can't stress enough that this is *your* quilt, and so you can do what you want with it.

3½″ squares made to fill a space

2. Stitch the blocks together in large, evenly sized modules if possible, and then in rows. If some of the blocks will not fit easily into a module or strip, do not panic! Follow the same instructions as in Borders as Design Elements (page 19).
3. Pin carefully to match seams where possible, and stitch the rows together.

Borders

This quilt has 4 blocks extending into the border.

1. Measure each section of your quilt and cut border strips to fit, using the 4 border strips.

2. Following the instructions in Borders as Design Elements (page 19), pin and stitch the borders to the quilt.

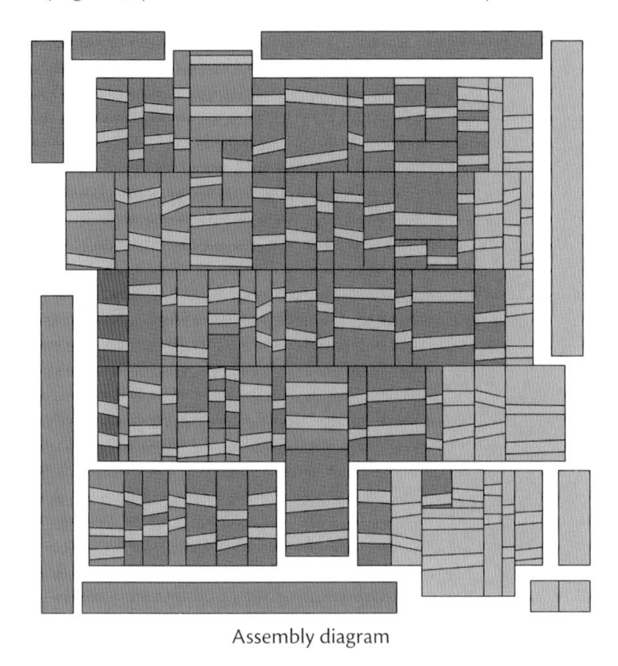

Assembly diagram

FINISHING

1. Refer to Quiltmaking Basics (page 74) to layer and baste your quilt to prepare it for quilting.

2. Quilt as desired. For this quilt, an allover design was machine quilted. Another option would be to free-motion quilt in a design highlighting the diagonal strips.

3. This quilt has a facing instead of a binding. Use the 5 strips of 3″-wide facing fabric and refer to Quiltmaking Basics to finish your quilt.

Gallery

These pages feature additional quilts that use the multiple block technique in different ways. All the fabrics were hand dyed by the author.

This quilt features two blocks and a proportionally correct spacer block.

Partytime, 54″ × 78″, designed, pieced, and quilted by Lisa Walton, 2010

Detail of *Partytime*

Breaking the Drought, 48″ × 68″, designed, embellished, pieced, and quilted by Lisa Walton, 2004

The fabrics for this quilt were embellished with trims and then cut into 8″ and 4″ finished squares and 4″ × 8″ finished rectangles. Squares and rectangles were placed randomly.

Detail of *Breaking the Drought*

Criss Cross Mayhem 63″ × 81″, designed, pieced, and quilted by Lisa Walton, 2005

A gradation of hand-dyed fabrics gives this quilt harmony; the basic quilt block is used in two sizes, with the small version in the border.

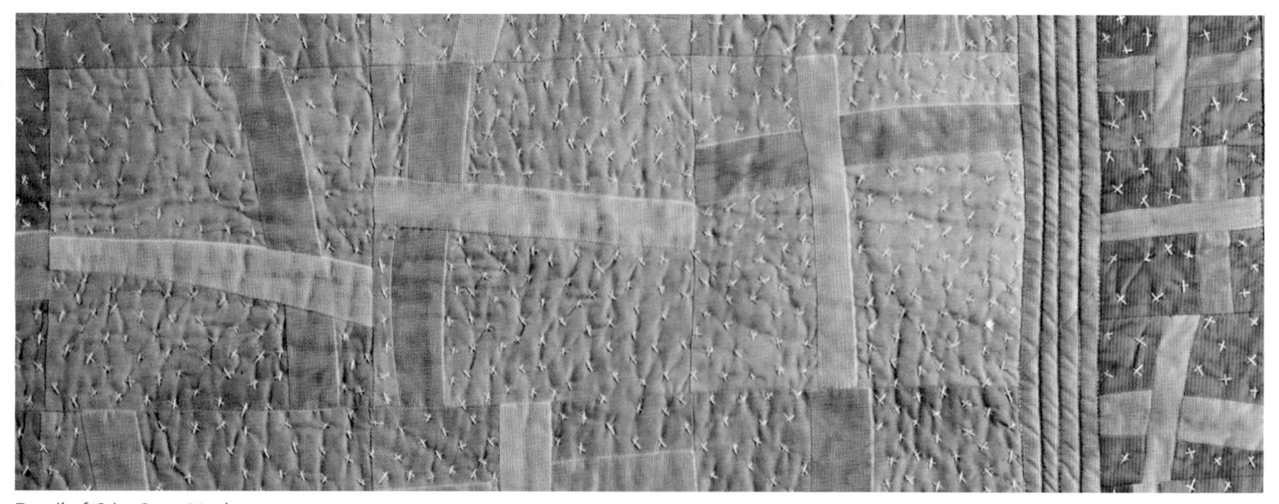

Detail of *Criss Cross Mayhem*

Deep Purple, 68″ × 68″, designed, pieced, and quilted by Lisa Walton, 2010

This quilt was made with just two pieces of hand-painted fabric. The same block is used throughout the quilt in increasing sizes. Appliquéd shapes of hand-dyed silk organza add an extra dimension. Appliquéd shapes were cut using an AccuQuilt Studio Fabric Cutter and Arabesque dies by Ricky Tims.

Detail of *Deep Purple*

Quiltmaking Basics

If you are a beginning quilter or need a refresher course, you can find some basic information in this chapter, but this is just a quick overview. For more information, consult a good basic quiltmaking book such as *The Practical Guide to Patchwork* by Elizabeth Hartman, available from Stash Books, an imprint of C&T Publishing, or *Start Quilting with Alex Anderson*, from C&T Publishing.

Tools and Supplies

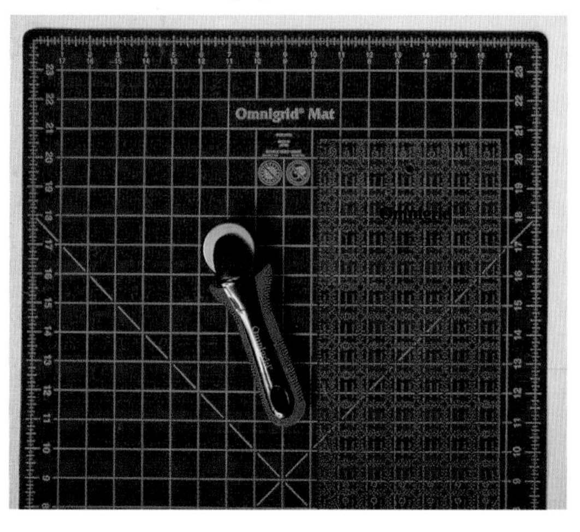

Basic tools

Use high-quality tools. You will use your basic tools all the time, and you get what you pay for. It is especially important to have a high-quality rotary cutter and mat, as well as clear plastic quilting rulers. Be sure you always have a sharp new blade in your rotary cutter so that it will cut safely and accurately.

Tip

The ruler is usually a little more accurate than the mat, so always take measurements with the ruler.

Thread

I love beautiful threads!

For piecing, I like to use 50-weight cotton thread. I use the same weight in the top thread and the bobbin. This weight tends to disappear into the fabric for a better finish.

Use a neutral thread, trying to match the same color family as the fabrics. It will blend better.

For quilting, thread weight depends on the effect you are trying to achieve. If you want the quilting to disappear into the fabric so that all you see is the texture the quilting creates, then use a finer thread. Some heirloom quilting in which you can hardly see the stitches is done with 100-weight silk thread.

If you want to see the thread, use a heavier-weight thread like a 28 weight or even a 12 weight.

Basic Patchwork Techniques

These are some simple guidelines to assist you when you are making a quilt, but nothing is written in stone. Despite popular belief, there are no "quilt police"—unless you are planning to try for Best of Show. We all do things differently, and you will find the best way for you. Just enjoy the process, and take pleasure in creating a quilt that is original and unique.

Piecing

- Unless stated, all fabric for the projects in this book is cut across the width of the fabric.
- All seams are a scant ¼"; this means a thread or two less than ¼".
- If you are using solid fabrics, batiks, or hand-dyed fabrics, it doesn't matter how you lay your fabrics together because there is no right or wrong side. However, if you are using printed fabric you will need to always stitch seams with the right sides together.
- When stitching seams, pin wherever two seams meet in order to line up the pieces accurately.
- Always press the seam allowance toward the darker fabric to prevent it from being seen through the top.

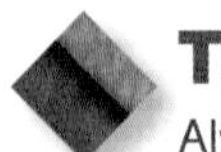

Tip

Always make up at least one block in each size to confirm the cutting dimensions and piecing technique. Nothing is worse than cutting up all your fabric and then finding you have made a mistake. Remember the saying "Measure twice, cut once."

Machine quilting

Before you begin quilting, always ensure that the backing and batting are at least 6" larger all around than the quilt top. This will allow for shrinkage when quilting.

Preparation

For all three layers of your quilt to be evenly quilted with no ripples or pleats, they need to be securely attached by basting through all three layers. Basting can be done by hand stitching, with pins, or with basting spray.

For machine quilting, I prefer pinning with safety pins because these can be taken out as you approach them on the sewing machine. Thread basting can sometimes get in the way, and if you stitch through it while quilting, the quilting stitch can break when the basting is removed.

Some quilters always use a spray glue specially formulated for basting, but this is not my preference.

1. Lay the backing fabric wrong side facing up on a table or floor, and tape it evenly on all sides so that it is taut but not stretched.
2. Lay the batting on top gently, and smooth it out so that it lies flat.
3. Lay the quilt top right side up on top of the batting, and tape it into place evenly on all sides, as you did for the backing.
4. Pin evenly all over the quilt top, ensuring that you have gone through all three layers. As a general guide, pins should be placed no further apart than a hand span or fist to ensure little movement.

Quilting on a domestic sewing machine

On a home machine, you can use a walking foot to quilt straight lines, or an embroidery or darning foot for free-motion quilting. For information on the specifics of machine quilting, consult a book such as *Foolproof Machine Quilting* by Mary Mashuta, available from C&T Publishing.

STRAIGHT-LINE QUILTING

When you are quilting straight-line designs, you need to ensure that all three layers of the quilt move under the needle at the same rate. This is achieved by using a walking foot, an attachment that most modern machines have. The stitches can be set at a specific length and will be even throughout the quilt.

You can also use a walking foot to accentuate blocks by stitching exactly in the seamlines (stich in-the-ditch).

Straight-line quilting with walking foot

FREE-MOTION QUILTING

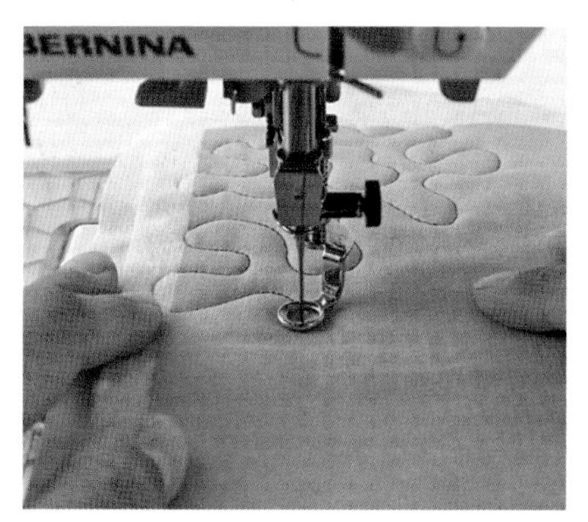

Free-motion quilting with darning foot

Free-motion quilting is a bit like drawing on the quilt with thread. You use an embroidery or darning foot and lower the feed dogs—the mechanisms that move fabric in conjunction with the needle to create even stitching. Instead of the quilt layers being fed under the needle, the movement is created by the quilter. Practice is required to achieve even stitching, but the reward is creating interesting free-form designs.

Tip

Sewing machine manufacturers are now making machines with larger harps—the area between the needle and the machine—especially for the home-quilting market. They make quilting larger quilts much easier.

Commercial quilting

Sending your quilt out to a fee-for-service quilter costs money, but it is often worth it to get your quilt done! Most commercial quilters use a large longarm or slightly smaller midarm machine. The quilt is attached to rollers on these machines, and the machine head moves across the surface to quilt it.

Two main types of quilting are available from commercial quilters.

Edge-to-edge quilting is done with premade patterns called pantographs, which are usually continuous-line designs that the quilter follows to create a repeat design over the entire quilt. This is generally the less expensive option because it can usually be done fairly quickly by an experienced quilter.

Custom quilting is usually the most expensive option because the quilter "draws" the designs with the machine. Depending on the skill of the quilter, this technique can create the most magnificent original designs.

Custom quilting by Nic Bridges

Finishing the Quilt

The two most common ways to finish the edge of a quilt are binding and facing. A wide variety of methods can be used; here I will show you the methods I use and am most comfortable with.

Binding

A binding creates a narrow frame around the quilt as well as finishing the edges. My preferred finished binding width is usually ¼″.

Calculating fabric quantity

1. Measure the length and width of the trimmed quilt.
2. Double this measurement and add about 30″ to allow for the corners and the overlap required at the join.

3. Divide the measurement by the width of the binding fabric. This will give you the number of strips required.

4. Multiply this number by 2¼″ (the binding width) to get the amount of fabric required. This width will result in a scant ¼″ finished binding.

Sewing method

1. Cut the required number of 2¼″ strips across the width of the fabric as required for the size of the quilt.

2. Sew the strips together end to end, using diagonal seams.

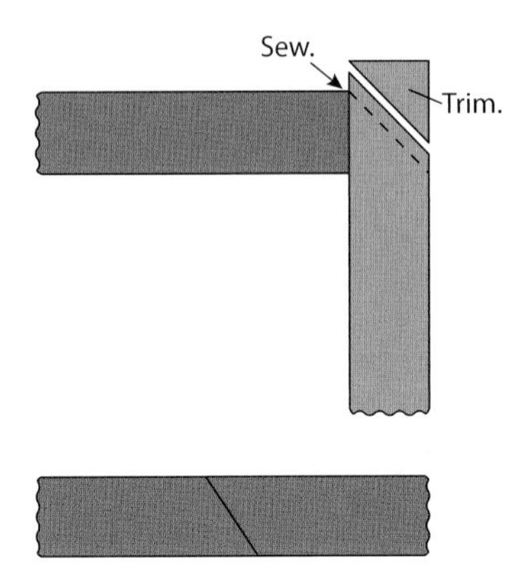

Tip

If you wish to add a hanging sleeve, prepare and pin it to the edge of the quilt before attaching the binding. Cut a strip of fabric about 8″ × the width of the quilt. Machine stitch a hem on each short edge. Fold in half lengthwise with the wrong sides together and press. Match the raw edges of the hanging sleeve with the edges of the quilt, pin, and sew it to the quilt when you stitch the binding.

3. Fold the binding strip lengthwise with wrong sides together as you sew it to the quilt.

4. Match the raw edges of the binding to the quilt edges. Using a ¼″ seam, start sewing about 5″ from the end of the strip, and stop ¼″ before the corner.

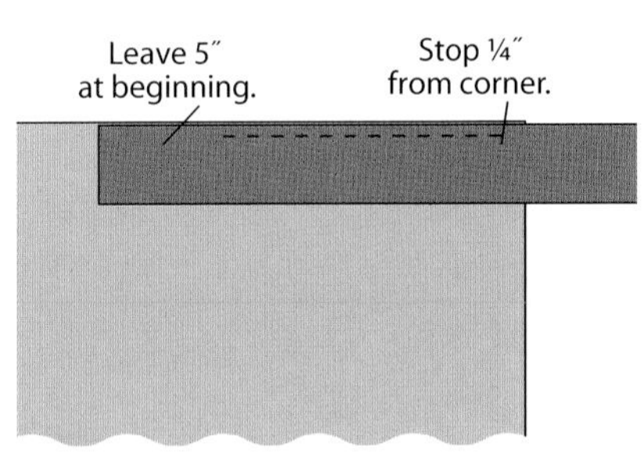

5. Fold the strip up, forming a 45° angle. Next fold the strip back down, and sew from the edge to ¼″ from the next corner. Repeat on all 4 corners until you are back at the first edge.

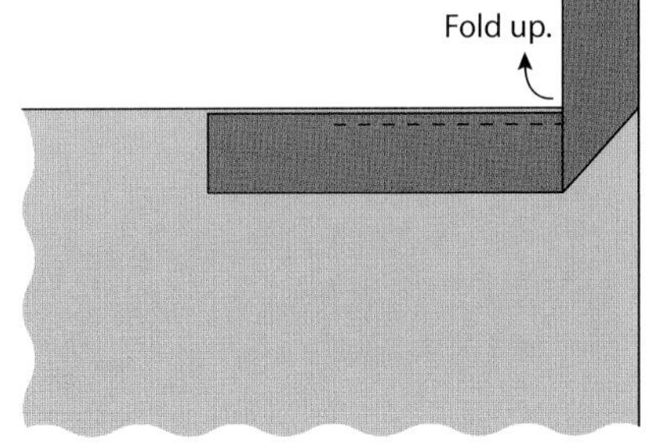

6. Meet the ends of the binding strips so they overlap by 2¼″. Unfold the ends of the binding strips. Put them right sides together and sew a diagonal seam.

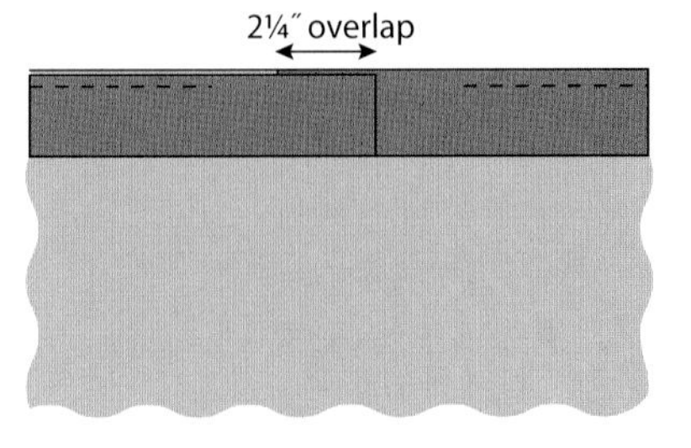

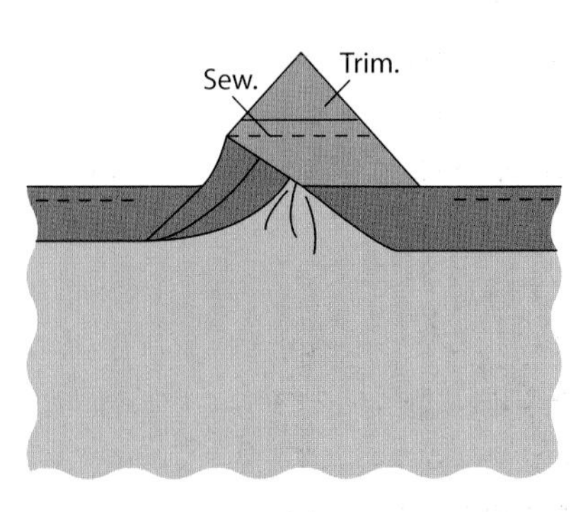

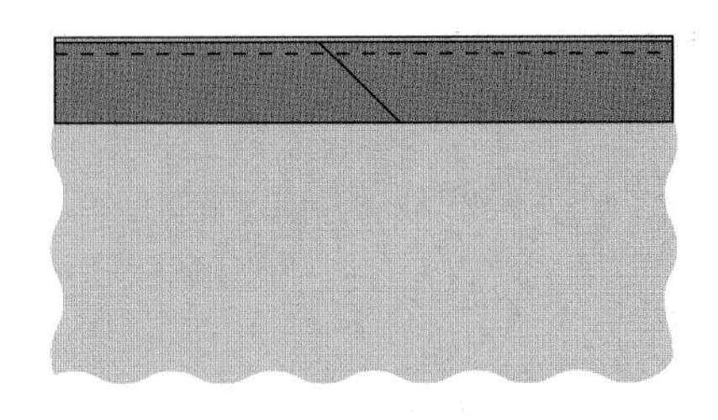

Facing

Facing finishes create a sharper edge to a quilt and are very useful when the design of your quilt would look better without a frame. Many art quilts use this technique to provide a crisp finish to the design.

1. Measure the sides, top, and bottom of the quilt.

2. Cut 3″ strips across the width of the fabric as required for the perimeter of the quilt. If the quilt is narrower than the strip length, join the strips at right angles.

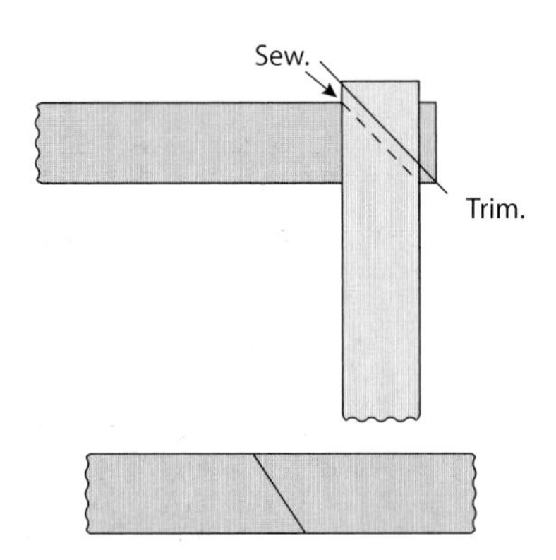

3. Cut 2 strips 1″ less than the width of the quilt for the top and bottom facing, and 2 strips 1″ longer than the side lengths for the sides.

4. Fold the facing strips lengthwise with wrong sides together.

5. Pin shorter lengths of the facings to the front of the top and bottom of the quilt top, with raw edges matching. Stitch with a ¼″ seam.

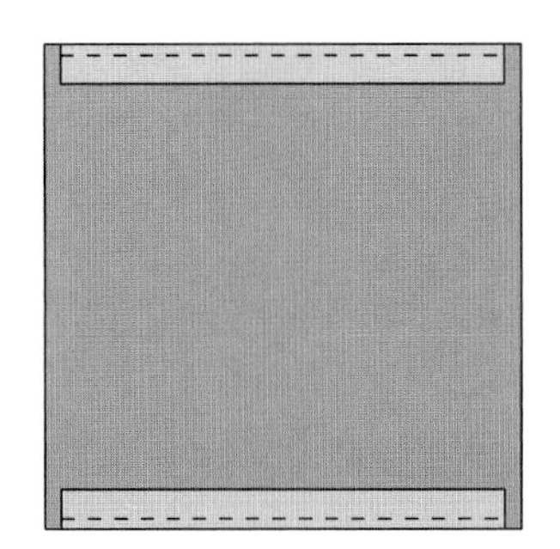

6. Fold out the top and bottom facings, and pin the longer lengths of the facings to the front of the quilt top. Stitch in-the-ditch of the previously sewn seams and then down the full length and across the seam at the other side. Trim across the corners.

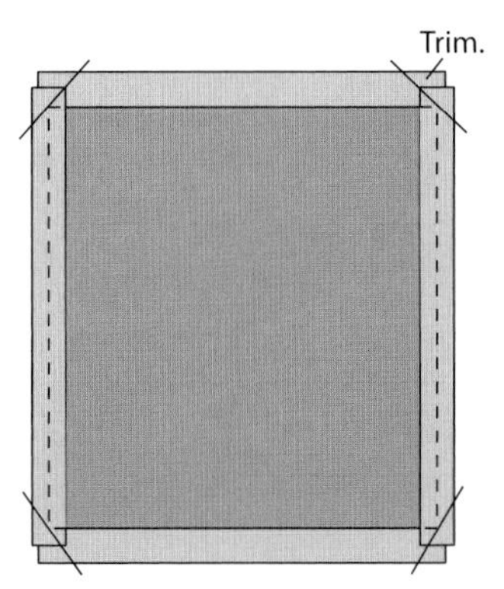

7. Fold the facings to the back of the quilt. Press gently with an iron.

8. Slipstitch in place.

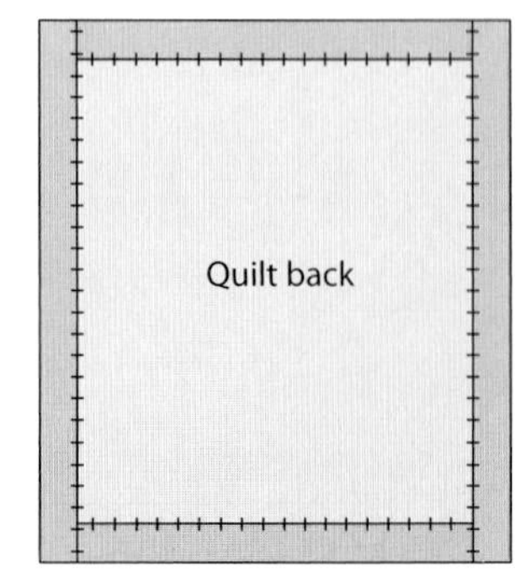

Fabrics drying in Lisa's garden

Resources

Batting

Matilda's Own
www.victoriantextiles.com.au

Pellon
www.pellonprojects.com

Dyes

PRO Chemical & Dye
www.prochemical.com

Dharma Trading Company
www.dharmatrading.com

Fabrics

Dyed & Gone to Heaven
www.dyedheaven.com

Robert Kaufman
www.robertkaufman.com

Graph paper

Harriet Hargrave's Quilter's Graph Paper
www.ctpub.com

Online graph paper
www.incompetech.com/graphpaper

Tools

Omnigrid
www.dritz.com/brands/omnigrid

The Electric Quilt Company
www.electricquilt.com

Thread

Aurifil
www.aurifil.com

About the Author

Photo by Peter Walton

Lisa Walton has been quilting for more than twenty years. Her first quilt was a disaster because she didn't realize that all the templates needed an additional ¼″ seam allowance. Not the best start for a Mariner's Compass quilt! However, she returned to quilting many years later when a friend helped her make a quilt from charm squares (it ultimately ended up as a dog quilt). Today, Lisa's award-winning quilts have been published in many magazines.

Lisa's passion for hand-dyed fabric was inspired by the serendipitous nature of the fabrics she began dyeing. With her husband, Peter, she started a business called Dyed & Gone to Heaven, which now produces a rainbow of fabric colors and styles.

She continues to develop her quilt style and now includes textures and surface design techniques with her hand-dyed fabrics as well as commercial fabrics to create unique, colorful quilts.

Lisa's love of teaching has taken her all over the world. In 2010 she was awarded the Jewel Pearce Patterson Scholarship for Quilting Teachers by the International Quilt Association in Houston, Texas.

Lisa lives in Sydney, Australia, with her long-suffering husband and more fabric than she will ever use.

For a list of other fine books from C&T Publishing, visit our website to view our catalog online.

C&T PUBLISHING, INC.
P.O. Box 1456
Lafayette, CA 94549
800-284-1114
Email: ctinfo@ctpub.com
Website: www.ctpub.com

C&T Publishing's professional photography services are now available to the public. Visit us at www.ctmediaservices.com.

Tips and Techniques can be found at www.ctpub.com > Consumer

For quilting supplies:

COTTON PATCH
1025 Brown Ave.
Lafayette, CA 94549
Store: 925-284-1177
Mail order: 925-283-7883
Email: CottonPa@aol.com
Website: www.quiltusa.com

Note: Fabrics shown may not be currently available, as fabric manufacturers keep most fabrics in print for only a short time.